101 THINGS TO DO & PLACES TO SEE IN

Saint Lucia

2016 EDITION

Russell Streeter

Author: Russell Streeter
Contributors: Stephane Terzuoli, Nelliane St Clair

Published by Caribbean Travel Guides Limited
Hampshire, United Kingdom
www.101thingstodoandsee.com

FREE EBOOK

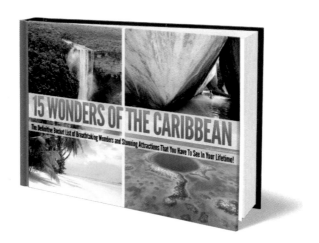

The Definitive Bucket List of Breath-taking Wonders & Stunning Attractions You Have To See In Your Lifetime!

This colourful and informative ebook tells the stories of 15 unique attractions from islands and countries around the Caribbean, accompanied by more than 25 full-colour pictures and a map, so you can start planning you next trip right away!

"Very beautiful and fascinating! Some of them have definitely been added to my bucket list!"
- A Gray

Table of Contents

Introduction   5

A Brief History of Saint Lucia   6

Chapter 1 Attractions (Numbers 1-55)   7

Chapter 2 Beaches (Numbers 56-82)   46

Chapter 3 Activities (Numbers 83-101)   65

Appendix I – Food & Drink   75

Appendix II – Scuba Diving Sites   80

Appendix III – List of Tour Operators   88

About the Author   90

FREE UPDATES

Things change slowly in Paradise – that's one of its attractions (and frustrations!). Still, over time attractions close, beaches change, activities are removed...and new ones take their place.

I could easily update the book next year and ask you pay again. But I'm not going to do that. Instead, I am offering to provide you with details of the updates I make to future editions, absolutely free.

You will receive updates for as long as this book is independently published. (I can't make promises on behalf of any future publishers.)

All you need to do is enter your email address here:

www.101thingstodoandsee.com/saint-lucia-free-updates

Introduction

The island that launched a thousand ships!

With her romantic beaches, geological wonders and lush tropical flora, Saint Lucia is worthy of comparison with Helen of Troy!

There is so much that commends this island as a holiday destination: the world's only drive-on volcano, romantic beaches of both brown and white sand, unspoilt rainforest and some of the best scuba diving in the region.

Her famous Pitons are a UNESCO World Heritage site and have been named as one of the world's top five must-see spectacles, while her dramatic land and seascapes continue to provide ideal settings for films and reality shows.

Visit Morne Fortuné and be transported back to a time when the British and French faced battled with musket and canon for the Island's treasures. Wallow in the warm mineral baths that are said to relieve rheumatism, sore joints and stress. And sample the local cuisine, a delicious blend of African, European and Amerindian influences.

How to use this book

Saint Lucia is too beautiful to spend your whole holiday lying on the beach or stuck in the hotel. This book provides enough information to make the most of your short time in this island paradise, with details of top attractions, beaches and activities.

Plan ahead by reading it in the departure lounge or on the plane, or take each day as it comes – the choice is yours. With maps, addresses and contact information for many of the island's tour guides and activity providers, your only challenge will be deciding which of her many wonders to leave until next time!

Russell Streeter

A Brief History of Saint Lucia

The first inhabitants of this beautiful island were the Arawaks who canoed their way across from South America around 200 A.D. About six hundred years later they were conquered by the fierce Caribs. These early Saint Lucians called the island Ioüanalao, meaning 'Land of the Iguanas' in the language of the Caribs, due to the island's large population of iguanas.

For many years it was believed that the first European to "discover" the island was Christopher Columbus in 1502, but recent evidence suggests that it was Juan de la Cosa, Columbus' former navigator, who actually first set foot on the island back in 1499. The Spanish did not settle on the island. In the 1500s the peg legged French pirate François le Clerc used Pigeon Island as a hideout.

The Dutch set up a base in Vieux Fort at the southern tip of the island in 1600. The first (attempted) settlement came in 1605 when a British ship was blown off course and sixty-seven colonists came ashore. But after five weeks forty-eight of them had died due to disease and conflict with the Caribs and the rest fled the island in a canoe! In 1639 a second attempt by the British to colonise the island also failed.

"Seven times British, seven times French" is a statement used to reflect the near-perpetual conflict between the British and the French between 1674 and 1814. Neither the French nor British were willing to surrender, as they knew the wealth that this island held, not just in natural beauty but also the island's natural deep-water harbours that offered protection for military vessels and also served as an ideal location for monitoring enemy military movements.

The island was finally ceded to the British 1814. Saint Lucia became independent in 1979, as a constitutional monarchy with the British monarch as the head of state and remains part of the Commonwealth.

CHAPTER 1
Attractions

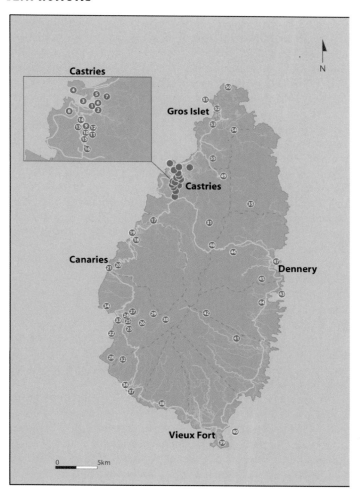

1. Derek Walcott Square

Right in the heart of Castries, the Derek Walcott Square is a great starting point for a walking tour of Saint Lucia's Capital. Bordered by the Basilica of the Immaculate Conception and by the National Public Library, it was originally the location of Castries Market. In 1892, the market was moved to Jeremie Street and Columbus Square was established in its place. Finally in 1993 it was renamed after Derek Walcott, winner of the Nobel Prize for Literature the previous year. Derek Walcott, born in Saint Lucia in 1930, still lives on the island.

As visitors stroll around the Square, a plaque honouring Derek Walcott with a verse from his epic poem sits steps away from another plaque in memory of another Saint Lucian Sir William Arthur Lewis (1915-79), winner of the Nobel Prize for Economics in 1979. There is also a monument in memory of the Great Wars' sacrifice. Lastly, (but predating the other occupants!) the most magnificent resident of the Derek Walcott Square is known as the "Massav" tree and is said to be over 400 years old.

2. Basilica of the Immaculate Conception

The majority of the population of Saint Lucia are Roman Catholic, a testament to its history and heritage, dating back to the island's days as a French colonial territory. Consequently, there is a Catholic church for every village and city on the island. And the largest church on the island – indeed, the largest in the Caribbean – sits adjacent to the Derek Walcott Square in Castries.

A church was built on the site in 1767. Following various construction projects to maintain the structure and add on to the building, the cathedral was finally completed in 1897. Named after Mary, mother of Jesus, under her title "Our Lady of the Immaculate Conception", the cathedral measures 61 metres (200 feet) long and 30 metres (100 feet) wide.

On 11th May 1999, it was elevated to the status of a Minor Basilica as part of the centenary celebrations.

The neat rows of polished wooden pews can accommodate over 2,000 worshippers and on 7th July 1986, Pope John Paul II performed a mass at maximum capacity gathering during his official visit to the island. Directly above the altar the island's patron Saint Lucia is portrayed. The late Dunstan St. Omer, celebrated local artist, decorated the cathedral with a colourful mural incorporating both Caribbean and African influences. Using bright red, green and yellow tones, it features the image of a "Black Madonna and Child".

This historical monument is open every day to the public from dawn to dusk, and is a must-see when visiting Castries. Attending mass remains the best way to enjoy a local experience among Saint Lucians. Weekend masses are scheduled on Saturdays at 8:00 am, and on Sundays at 6:00 am, 8:00 am and 10:30am.

Address: Micoud St. & Laborie St., Castries
Telephone: +758-452-2271/72

3. Port Castries

The fortunes of Castries have always been influenced by the port's activities. The first adventurers used the bay as a safe refuge and the French found it convenient for anchoring and mending their ships. Their first settlement was called La Carenage. This facility gave Castries its motto: "Statio Haud Malefida Carinis", or a "Safe Harbour for Ships". Port Castries, used as a coaling station for nearly 100 years, has also been used for ship repairs and commercial warehouse storage.

Castries Harbour is now much smaller than before, but it has become a major cruise ship port. Tourism and retail are now the main commercial activities in the city, with an expanded port capable of holding up to 5 large cruise ships simultaneously. Both terminals described here offer Duty Free shopping centres featuring a range of local and imported products.

La Place Carenage is an air-conditioned Duty Free shopping complex on the Castries waterfront. Pointe Seraphine is located on the other side of Castries Harbour, and comprises an open-air complex of Duty Free boutiques and a tourist information centre – a good spot to check all the tours available in Saint Lucia.

4. Meadows Battery

Meadows Battery is located on the Vigie Peninsula, a small piece of land to the north of Port Castries. Vigie means "look out" in French and the British built the battery in 1898 to defend the island against French attacks — a constant threat with the island of Martinique a mere 50 kilometres or so to the north.

The buildings are abandoned and the site is not a regular tourist spot, but if you have your own transportation it's easy enough to find.

The peninsula is also home to the National Archives, the French and Venezuelan Embassies, Saint Mary's College, the Residence of the Archbishop of Castries and the offices of the Archdiocese of Castries.

You could combine your visit with a dip in the sea at Vigie Beach.

Meadows Battery

5. Serenity Park

Situated on Castries Waterfront, between the Fisheries and the Government Buildings stretch, Serenity Park was officially opened to the public on 15th May 2011, by the Governor-General Dame Pearlette Louisy, the Minister of Local Government Richard Frederick and Prime Minister, the Honourable Stephenson King.

The name of the park was submitted by students of the R.C. Boys Infant School, winner of a competition amongst the schools in the Castries basin. The park was designed and built by local professionals — in particular young professionals just starting their construction related professions.

6. Constitution Park

Constitution Park is a block away from the Basilica of the Immaculate Conception, between the High Court House and the House of Assembly. On 21st February 2014, ahead of Saint Lucia's 35th Independence Day, a 9-foot tall bronze statue was unveiled in honour of former Prime Minister, Sir John George Melvin Compton. Erected at the centre of Constitution Park, the statue, designed by Saint Lucian sculptor Ricky George, depicts Sir John facing the William Peter Boulevard, where he operated his private law office for many years.

The crowded ceremony was attended by Heads of State from St Vincent and the Grenadines and Grenada, Saint Lucia's Governor General, members of Cabinet and Parliament. It was a tribute to the first Prime Minister of Saint Lucia who gave over half a century of his life to public service, and died in 2007 during his last elected term.

7. Folk Research Centre

While English is the island's official language, a large portion of the population speaks Saint Lucian Creole French ("Creole" or "Kwéyòl"), a language that is primarily based on French, but with African and Carib influences. There are millions of creole speakers around the world, mostly in former French colonies, with each society developing its own unique version of the language.

Though Creole has been in use in the Caribbean for two hundred years, it was mainly an oral language and it was not until 1992 that a dictionary of Saint Lucia Creole was published*. In 2001 the Ministry of Education published the *Kwéyòl Dictionary*, the result of nearly two decades of research. For over 40 years Saint Lucia's Folk Research Centre (FRC) has been promoting the study of, and interest in the island's Creole language, heritage and culture.

Part study centre, part museum, the FRC also runs Creole language classes and houses an extensive library of publications, recordings and photographs.

In August 1999 the FRC was granted Development Agency Status and its headquarters' classified as a National Heritage site.

Yet Creole culture is not just limited to language but includes food, music, art and other folk traditions.

* *Dictionary of Saint Lucia Creole* (1992) James E. Mondesir, ed. by Lawrence D. Carrington

The celebration of this culture reaches a peak in October with International Creole Month and since 1984 Saint Lucians have celebrated Jounen Kwéyòl (Creole Day) on the last Sunday of October.

The FRC is open Monday to Friday from 8:30am to 4:30pm. Address: Mount Pleasant, Castries
Telephone: +758-452-2279, 453-1477 or 285-0340
Website: www.stluciafolk.org

Constitution Park, Castries

8. La Toc Battery

La Toc Battery is one of the islands' best-preserved stockades, built by the British in 1888 on a hillside overlooking Castries Harbour and out into the Caribbean Sea.

The hilltop gun emplacement was designed to protect the harbour, which could hold the entire British Navy — the largest British port in the Caribbean. With its thick, reinforced walls and mysterious underground corridors, it is British engineering at its finest.

tour of this fascinating historical site will take you back in time to the violent colonial times when the British and French fought repeatedly over the island. The museum contains old maps, uniforms, guns and gun shells, but the highlight is the 18-tonne rifled muzzle-loader cannon.

The site is managed by the owner of Bagshaws Saint Lucia, a local silk screen-printing manufacturer and outlet, situated below La Toc Battery. Visits are by appointment only, but La Toc is also visited by tour operators (see Appendix III).

Address: La Toc Road, Castries

Telephone: +758-452-7921 or 452-6039

Website: www.st-lucia-vacation-guide.com/bagshaws-st-lucia.html

9. Morne Fortuné/Fort Charlotte

Morne Fortuné is the summit of a ridge rising to 260 metres (852 feet) above sea level. From La Toc Battery, follow the road that snakes up Morne Fortuné's slopes in order to reach the 18th and 19th centuries' most heavily fought-over sites in the Caribbean. This journey to the top offers multiple photo opportunities, with spectacular views of Castries Harbour, Vigie's Lighthouse, Rat Island and even Pigeon Point in the north of the island and the Pitons in the south. On a clear day you can see all the way to Martinique.

The French began using Morne Fortuné as a military base after 1768. The name means "Hill of Good luck", although it was not so lucky for the thousands of soldiers who died in bloody battles between the French and the British.

It was renamed Fort Charlotte by Prince Edward of Britain (son of King George III and father of Queen Victoria) following a victorious battle in 1794.

The most famous battle took place on 24th May 1796. The Royal Inniskilling Fusiliers captured the Morné from the French after an epic uphill battle. A monument was erected in memory of the fallen soldiers. Numerous gun emplacements and cannons are still visible around the area, such as the Four Apostles Battery.

In recent years, following the restoration of several military buildings, the site was converted into Sir Arthur Lewis Community College, named after the Saint Lucian scholar who was awarded the Nobel Prize for Economics in 1979. He is buried in the College grounds. Morne Fortuné also hosts the Saint Lucian campus of the University of the West Indies.

The many historical buildings and military sites on Morne Fortuné are vested to the Saint Lucia National Trust for preservation. They are open to public access at all times, but booking one of Morne Fortuné's packaged tours is the best and easiest way to explore the area. For more information, contact the Saint Lucia National Trust.

Telephone: +758-452-5005
Website: www.slunatrust.org

Scattered around the slopes of Morne Fortuné, a wide choice of attractions is available for you to discover, as described in numbers 10 through 14 below.

10. The Powder Magazine and Guard Cells

These are the oldest remaining buildings on Morne Fortuné, dating back to 1765. The Powder Magazine was used for storing gunpowder and ammunitions; you can see that the walls were built very thick, in case any accidental explosions. The Guard Cells were used as jail for soldiers.

11. The French and British Cemeteries

The military cemetery at Morne Fortuné was established over 250 years ago and is the final resting place for British and French soldiers, as well as their families and other civilians. Two unnamed tombs are all that remain of the French cemetery, while the oldest named grave belongs to Emilia Wood who died in 1810. There are mass graves of people who died from yellow fever and other epidemics to which the population was so vulnerable in the 18th and 19th centuries.

The cemetery contains the graves of several of the men and women who fought on behalf of Saint Lucia during the first and second world wars, as well as past governors of Saint Lucia. The last Governor to be buried there was Sir Ira Simmons in 1974.

12. Inniskilling Fusiliers Monument

The 27th (Inniskilling) Regiment of Foot was formed in Ireland in 1689, and was first posted in the West Indies in 1701. They fought against the French in North America and the West Indies during the Seven Year's War (1756-1763) and again during the American War of Independence (1775-1783).

The Regiment helped capture Saint Lucia from the French in 1778, but the island was later returned to France. In 1796 the Regiment was again part of a force that besieged the island and defeated the French. The leader of those forces, General Abercrombie, was so impressed by bravery of the 27th Regiment that he allowed their Colours to be flown for an hour before the Union Flag. The Inniskilling Monument is located in the grounds of the Sir Arthur Lewis Community College.

13. Four Apostles Battery

Officially named the Morne Battery by the War Office, it is situated above the eastern side of Morne Road. The construction of the battery was completed on the 31st of July 1892. It is referred to as the Four Apostles Battery in memory of a quartet of grim muzzle-loading cannon once mounted on the site. The four cannon were recently excavated and are being restored to their former glory, as part of an overall development plan for this historic area.

14. Prevost Redoubt

Named after General Prevost, Lieutenant Governor of the island from 1798 to 1802, this was an ideal lookout point from which to survey Castries harbour, the Vigie peninsula and all the way to Pigeon Island. Men were stationed here with muskets, to look out for approaching invaders.

15. Caribelle Batik

High up on the hillside, with a spectacular view of the city of Castries, stands Caribelle Batik where Saint Lucians continue the ancient practice of fabric art. Craftsmen and women take plain fabrics and adorn them with the most vibrant colours, using batik and screen-printing techniques. Next, skilled seamstresses turn the fabric into clothing, accessories, wall hangings and more. (Fancy a colourful sarong or shirt for your trip to the beach?) Take a tour of the studio and witness first hand the production of these fine creations.

A little further on the same road, the historic century-old Government House is still the official residence of the Governor General, and is an outstanding piece of Victorian architecture, housing a museum called "Le Pavillon Royal" on its grounds.

Address: Howelton House, Old Victoria Road, The Morne, Castries

Telephone: +758-452-3785

Website: www.caribellebatikstlucia.com

Inniskilling Fusiliers Monument

16. Eudovic's Art Studio

Situated on the south side of Morne Fortuné, Eudovic's Art Studio was established in 1975 by Joseph Eudovic, at the time already a well-known wood sculptor and teacher of arts and crafts. Forty years on the Studio is still producing works of art using teak, cedar and mahogany.

However, the main wood used is from the laurier canelle tree. Although this tree is now extinct in Saint Lucia, Eudovic uses old roots and stumps found in the forests around the island. Thus each piece is influenced by the unique shape and characteristics of the foraged raw materials.

These days Eudovic works with a team of sculptors, artisan and staff. Don't worry about how to fit a sculpture in your suitcase: they will pack and ship all purchases to you on request! Some Morne Fortuné tours include a visit to Eudovic's Art Studio.

Address: Goodlands, Castries

Telephone: +758-452-2747

Website: www.eudovicart.com

17. Roseau Valley Distillery

Located inside Roseau village on the West Coast Road, south of Castries, the small distillery is the property of the Saint Lucia Distillers Group, which boasts a range of over 25 rum and rum-related products, may of which have won international awards.

Lush green fields of banana trees and sugar cane surround the distillery and you can still see the old steel cranes that were once used to hoist sugar loads. These days molasses, the raw material for rum and a by-product of sugar production, is imported, mainly from Guyana.

If you've often wondered, while enjoying a refreshing rum punch by the pool, how the spirit is made, here is your chance to witness this fascinating process. The "Rhythm of Rum" tour lasts for an hour and available Monday to Fridays (except public holidays) with the first tour starting at 9am and the last at 3pm. If you can gather a group of 14 or more persons, the tour is available seven days a week.

As part of the tour you will be able to buy products at factory prices but, of course, you must be over 18 to purchase any of the alcoholic products.

Telephone: +758-456-3148 or 456-3192

Website: www.saintluciarums.com

Eudovic's Art Studio

18. La Sikwi Sugar Mill Plantation

Located along the Big Anse la Raye River, La Sikwi (Creole for sugar mill) sits in the gardens of a beautiful 400-acre plantation and features an on-site museum and a cultural theatre with a 40-foot (13-metre) tall water wheel.

The mill was built in 1860 when sugar cane production played a prominent role in the island's economy. Production started to decline in the late 19th century and many estates switched to bananas and cocoa. La Sikwi fell into disrepair but was renovated and restored as a tourist attraction in 1990.

The tour of the plantation takes you on a journey into the past, detailing the process for transforming cane juice into crude raw sugar and molasses. The gardens of the estate contain many types of flowers including hibiscus, heliconias,

birds of paradise and ginger lilies. Cocoa, mangos and ripe coconuts wait to be picked, and let's not forget the star of the estate: the sugar cane plants which grow tall and majestic.
Address: La Sikwi Sugar Mill Plantation, Anse la Raye
Telephone: +758-452-6323

19. Church of the Nativity of the Blessed Virgin Mary

For this one, we travel south along the west coast and the Caribbean Sea. With the big Anse la Raye river running along its south side, the Church of the Nativity of the Blessed Virgin Mary is located between the beach and the village's main street. Like all small coastal villages in Saint Lucia, fishing is the main occupation, and the Roman Catholic Church plays a central role in local life.

The church was first built in 1762. The wooden structure was destroyed in 1780 by a hurricane, and after being rebuilt, was destroyed by fire. Finally, the people of Anse la Raye provided the labour and the stones, and they completed the construction of the present church in 1907.

On the church's boundary wall, a mural (150 ft / 50 m long) illustrating scenes of the village's life was painted and donated by the St. Omer family.

Towering over the Parish ground, there is a large statue of Jesus on the Cross (20 ft / 6 m) standing at the front, and as we proceed into the church, we are welcomed by a statue of Mary over the entrance. Inside, the wooden pillars, the dark wood ceiling and the centre wall's mural contrast beautifully with the white stone altar imported from France.

Open to the public from dawn till dusk all week, the weekend mass is scheduled on Sundays at 10:00am.
Address: Church St., Anse la Raye
Telephone: +758-451-4227

20. Plas Kassav

Cassava is a root vegetable and a major source of carbohydrates for around 500 million people in tropical regions around the world; Saint Lucia is no exception. The sweet variety of cassava can be eaten raw or cooked, or made into flour that is gluten free. (There is also a bitter variety that must be cooked to remove toxins.)

Plas Kassav (Creole for Cassava Place) was set up in 1998 by Joan Henry as a means of supporting her family of nine children. Over the years the business has grown, now employs more than ten people, (including many of Joan's children), sells a range of plain and flavoured cassava breads and is the main cassava buyer for the local farmers.

Throughout this expansion Joan and her team have maintained traditional methods of production, making flour from the raw cassava, and baking that into bread, all in the same facility. It is both a cafe and a factory open for guided tours.

The range of flavoured unleavened cassava breads includes coconut, cherry and raisin, apple and raisin, cinnamon and more.

Address: Anse la Verdure, Canaries
Telephone: +758-459-4050

21. Anse la Liberte Camping and Heritage Site

On the west coast of Saint Lucia, situated near Canaries, this 133-acre (50 hectare) property was donated to the Saint Lucia National Trust in 1990 from the Nature Conservancy in the USA. The name 'Anse la Liberte' ("Bay of Freedom") was derived from the fact that the site was the venue for major celebrations by newly freed slaves.

With an undulating landscape featuring ridges and valleys, the site also comprises a small beach and the famous "Brigand" caves. Visitors will appreciate here the diversity of plant species with both dry scrub forest and rainforest habitats offering a variety of edible tropical fruits. Some 17 species of bird can be sighted early mornings and late afternoons.

For more information on visiting or camping contact the National Trust (+758-452-5005 or www.slunatrust.org).

22. The Pitons

Rated as Saint Lucia's top attraction, the world famous conical twin Pitons of Soufrière are the must-see landmark of the island. Rising up side by side from the sea, like the fossilised horns of some massive underwater creature, the Pitons were formed by volcanic activity around 250,000 years ago.

Gros Piton to the south is 770 metres high, while Petit Piton is a bit shorter at 743 metres. At least 148 plant species have been recorded on Gros Piton, and a further 97 on Petit Piton and the Piton Mitant Ridge. Gros Piton is home to 27 bird species, of which 5 are endemic, 3 indigenous rodents, one opossum, 3 bats, 8 reptiles and 3 amphibians.

The Pitons Management Area (2,909 hectares) was awarded World Heritage status by UNESCO in 2004.

You can visit any island in the Caribbean and hike any nature trail, but Petit Piton is in a class of its own. With steep trails and treacherous terrain, it is definitely an advanced hike.

Gros Piton is a more manageable climb, though a guide is required and it will take most of your day. Browse the tour operators at Appendix III or hire a guide at the trailhead.

However, most visitors simply view the Pitons from below for their scenic beauty, and the best panorama is from the Soufrière Hills.

See also Appendix II for scuba diving sites around the Pitons.

23. Sulphur Springs

Located just past Morne Coubaril Estate on a 45-hectare park, Caribbean's only drive-in volcano is the hottest and most active geothermal area in the Lesser Antilles. Formally known as the "Qualibou" by Amerindians (meaning "place of death") this true natural wonder was created by a major eruption 40,000 years ago.

A walk through the crater takes you past pools and hot springs bubbling with sulphuric steam. You can also bathe in warm pools downstream reputed for their soothing effects; the pungent aroma of sulphur can relieve pain or sinus congestion and leave you looking many years younger. My advice: bring a dark bathing suit along and enjoy a mud bath — great for your skin!

The Sulphur Springs' tour takes 30 minutes. The Park is open seven days a week from 9:00 am to 5:00 pm, including public holidays.

Address: Sulphur Springs, Soufrière
Telephone: +758-459-5726 / 7200 / 7686

24. Diamond Falls, Botanical Gardens

Less than a mile east of Soufrière, Diamond Falls and Botanical Gardens are situated on a multiple award-winning tourism site and are one of the natural wonders of Saint Lucia. Once a working plantation producing cocoa, limes and copra (the coconut kernel), this historical Estate has become a major tourist attraction that includes the Botanical Gardens, the Mineral Baths, a waterfall and a nature trail.

Considered a haven for birds and insects, Diamond Falls Botanical Gardens are naturally beautiful, brightened by all the flowering bushes and shrubs planted around and beneath taller existing trees. Due to the tropical climate, the exotic blossoms of Hibiscus, Ixora, Heliconia, Anthurium and Balisier can be enjoyed all year round. In existence since 1983, the well maintained paths of the Botanical Gardens winds through the Mineral Baths amidst ferns and banana plants to reach the spot where the Diamond River drops into a colourful waterfall.

The waterfall is approximately 17 metres (55 feet) high and is a mixture of rain and volcanic waters fed by the Sulphur Springs. Diamond Falls' waters are laced with minerals, contributing to the ever-changing kaleidoscope of colours.
Please note that due to major damages suffered during Hurricane Tomas, the nature trail is presently being repaired.
Address: Diamond Falls Botanical Gardens, Soufrière
Telephone: +758-459-7155
Website: www.diamondstlucia.com

25. Mineral Baths
Further downstream from the waterfall, the Mineral Baths were originally built in 1784 for the French troops to benefit from its therapeutic waters. They were destroyed not long after in the war that followed the French revolution, but were rebuilt in the 1980s and today are still fed from the steaming waters that so enchanted the French in the 18th century.

Three more pools, filled from the overflow of the original tanks, are situated in the open and the water is pleasantly warm. Bathing is said to be useful for people suffering from rheumatism, sore joints, painful muscles and stress. Locals boast that bathing in these waters makes you look ten years younger! Don't forget to bring a bathing suit.

26. Toraille Waterfall
Toraille is the easiest waterfall to access in Saint Lucia. Located in the small community of Fond St. Jacques, travel further east on the same road that leads to Diamond Falls and the Edmond Forest Reserve.

Diamond Falls

After passing through the entrance hut, where you pay the US$3.00 fee, it's just a short walk to reach the pool beneath the falls and take a dip. The Toraille Waterfall cascades down from a height of 15 metres (50 feet) at the centre of a landscaped garden. You can also wander along the small nature trail, through the lush greens and dazzling colours of this tropical paradise. Changing rooms are available, as well as a seating area for picnics. Midday is the best time for photos.

Address: Fond St. Jacques, Soufrière
Telephone: +758-459-7527 or 459-5415

27. New Jerusalem Mineral Baths

Situated along the Fond St. Jacques Road, the entrance to the New Jerusalem Baths is located further on from the Toraille Waterfall. To access these secluded hot and cold baths, follow the trail for a short ten-minute walk on the other side of the river. This site, usually not crowded, is a welcome retreat for sore muscles and back pains.

Owned and managed by local folks, it features two warm baths equipped with seating areas and three different temperatures of water flowing from bamboo faucets above. The pressure creates a nice warm body massage. You will enjoy the privacy and calm of the New Jerusalem Baths.

Address: Fond St. Jacques, Soufrière
Telephone: +758-518-9802

28. Gros Piton Nature Trail

The Gros Piton Nature Trail starts in the small village of Fond Gens Libres (which translated means "Valley of the Free People"), located east inland from the majestic Gros Piton peak. You will have to hire a taxi for the day to get there. The tour begins at the Interpretation Centre, where exhibits of rare vegetation and birds found along the trail are presented. There is a US$30.00 Permit Fee to be paid when you make arrangements for the guide.

Before starting the five hours round trip, get prepared: a backpack with 2-3 litres of water per person, good climbing shoes, energy food and short pants. The way is steep and wet, with boulders and roots scattered along the way.

The base of the trail winds around the mountain at a gradual slope, offering breathtaking views of Choiseul Village and the Caribbean Sea. The hike features caves, tunnels, rock shelters, several Brigand camps, signal stations, look-outs and landing sites. Anse l'Ivrogne Canyon can also be visited along the way. The second half of the trail involves a steep ascent to Gros Piton summit, with a height of 2,200 feet (798 metres), and is intended for adventurous hikers. Just imagine the view from the top!

Address: Gros Piton Nature Trail, Fond Gens Libres

Telephone: +758-486-1561, 717-8604

Website: www.grospiton.com

29. Mount Gimie Hike

The Mount Gimie Hike is one of the side trails available to visitors to the Edmund Forest Reserve. You will have to drive from Soufrière to Fond St. Jacques, passing through the village of Zenon, and continuing along until you reach the Forestry Department Ranger's Station. You will need a four-wheel drive to complete this hour-long journey. A US$40.00 fee per person is payable at the station.

The trail that leads to the highest point on the island, Mount Gimie (950 metres or 3,117 feet) is a tough trek and not often requested. Let the Forestry Department know beforehand so they can arrange a guide familiar with the route. The route takes you through the rainforest, which has an annual rainfall of 2,500-3,800 mm, so you may get wet! Bring a change of clothes just in case.

The Edmund Reserve's main trail goes through the Quilesse Forest Reserve and ends with the Des Cartiers Rain Forest Trail. It is not a difficult trek despite the length: 4 hours each way for 7 miles (10 km). It is part of the old French Road, which links the Caribbean side of the island (Soufrière) to the Atlantic side (Micoud). The trail is flat much of the way, with convenient footbridges for crossing the occasional stream.

This is the ideal trail for bird watchers. Five of the endemic bird species on the island, including the Jacquot (Amazona Versicolour), Saint Lucia's National Parrot and the Saint Lucian Oriole, are must-sees.

If you do walk to the other side, you'll either need to walk back or arrange in advance for a ride in Micoud. In any case, you must arrange for a guide in advance through the Forestry Department (+758-468-5645/5648/5649). Open Tuesday to Friday.

Address: Edmund Forest Reserve, Fond St. Jacques, Soufrière

Edmund Forest

30. Enbas Saut Waterfalls Trail

The Enbas Saut Waterfalls Trail is a 2.5 mile (5 km) cut trail, which takes around 2 hours to complete. Like all treks in the area, it features a combination of rainforest, cloud forest, woodlands and wildlife.

The Saint Lucian Parrot, the Saint Lucia Black Finch, the Blue Hooded Finch and other mountain whistlers are commonly spotted on this trail.

The trail is most famous for its two cascading waterfalls and pools at the head of Troumassee River. You will have to walk down scores of wooden steps before reaching them and enjoying a well-deserved bath. Bring some dry clothes.

The trail is also situated within the 19,000-acre Edmund Forest Reserve and you must arrange for a guide and pay the US$40.00 fee. Contact the Saint Lucia Forestry Department (+758-468-5645/5648/5649).

31. Piton Flore Hike

Located in the Forestiere community, 30 minutes' drive from Castries, the trail begins where the road ends, next to the Forestry Department Ranger Station. A US$40.00 fee per person is payable at the station.

A guide is not necessary but would still a good idea to complete this 4-hour round-trip. Much of the trail follows the 200-year-old Old French Road connecting Castries with Dennery. The 5 km (3 miles) long trail features an abundance of large and spectacular fig trees and ferns. The path is protected from the blazing sunshine by tall trees, some towering more than 30 metres (100 feet) above. As you reach the top of Piton Flore, you will have the best view onto the Cul-de-Sac Valley.

Open from Tuesday to Thursday. Contact the Saint Lucia Forestry Department (+758-468-5645/5648/5649).

32. Tet Paul Nature Trail

Located in the tropical forest of the Pitons Management Area in Soufrière, the Tet Paul Nature Trail takes about an hour to complete and is rated as easy to moderate. Visitors can learn about medicinal plants and trees, sample exotic tropical fruits and discover the traditional Amerindian art of cassava production. The highlight is the "stairway to heaven": steps leading up to a platform that offers a 360-degree panoramic view. On a clear day you can see all the way to Saint Vincent to the south and Martinique to the north.

The Tet Paul Nature Trail is open every day from 9:00 am to 5:00 pm, except on the first Friday in September. A small entry fee applies, with special rates for children. The tour is guided by friendly and knowledgeable locals. A small picnic area is available to the guests. Bring your camera!
Website: www.tetpaulnaturetrail.com

33. Morne Coubaril Estate

Overlooking Soufrière Bay, Morne Coubaril Estate is Saint Lucia's oldest French Creole Estate and has belonged to the same family for over 200 years. The 250-acre plantation produces cocoa, coffee and copra, as well as a selection of tropical fruits, including orange, grapefruit and lime.

Guests can participate in guided tours of the plantation, with its tropical gardens and replica of a traditional village featuring authentic huts. Guides will show you how coconuts are opened, roasted and used to process margarine, soaps, oil and animal feed. Cocoa is fermented, dried on racks in the sun, oiled, polished through the art of dancing on them, crushed and then formed into chocolate sticks. Cassava is grated, squeezed of excess water, dried over a fire and turned into flour. The tour ends with breathtaking views of the volcano.

For the more adventurous, zip lining activities over the estate are available, offering a panoramic view of the Pitons and the historical town of Soufrière.

After the tour, make sure to take a seat in the original Plantation House to enjoy a Creole meal prepared with seasonal local products from the plantation. Call for further information and bookings.
Address: Morne Coubaril Estate/ Saint Lucia Ziplining, Soufrière
Telephone: +758-712-5808
Website: www.stluciaziplining.com

34. Ruby Estate

Located just outside Soufrière, the Ruby Estate plantation has been the property of the Du Boulay family for four generations. The original Du Boulay family beach home on Soufrière Bay was refurbished into 'The Still Beach House', the perfect getaway for the traveller looking for a Creole experience in the cultural heartland of Saint Lucia. Ruby Estate supplies The Still Beach House Restaurant with fresh local products, the lumber for the bedrooms' furnishings and the tropical floral bouquets. A free tour of the plantation is offered to every guest. The estate features a functioning waterwheel, acres of citrus and cocoa cultivation, and copra processing for coconut oil and other by-products. The two-hour-long tour includes some hiking, along with fresh fruit and coconut tasting under the supervision and expertise of the Ruby Estate team.

Call the staff at The Still Beach House for further information on the plantation tours.

Address: Ruby Estate, Soufrière.

Telephone: +758-459-7620 or 717-5051

Website: www.soufrierebeachhouse.com

Sulphur Springs

35. Castries Waterworks Forest Reserve

Castries Waterworks Forest Reserve was established in 1916 to protect the water resources that supply the needs of the Castries area. You might say that it was an early form of environmental protection on the island! It is an excellent place to see many of Saint Luica's endemic species of bird, including the Saint Lucia amazon, the country's national bird. Located in the highland community of Chassin, between Piton Flore and La Sorciere mountain peak, it is just half an hour's drive from Castires.

Also located in the reserve, Rainforest Adventures gives visitors a unique way to see the rainforest: from up in the trees! Sail through air from tree to tree on their network of zip lines, or travel at a more leisurely pace in the aerial tram. Rainforest Adventures offers hiking and bird watching tours as well.

Telephone: +758-458-5151

Website: www.rainforestadventure.com/st-lucia

36. Our Lady of Lourdes Church

This beautiful Roman Catholic Church is located in Choiseul - you can't miss it, on the only bend of Choiseul's main street, squeezed between the mouth of the river and the beach.

If you get a chance to travel around Saint Lucia during your stay and if you reach all the way down to Choiseul (few tours go there), you must take a break in this small fishing village. Sample the "Fish Water" (local fish soup with the "catch of the day" — preferably served by an old lady called 'Mum' by all the locals, and right in her own kitchen of course!) and visit this iconic central landmark.

Building started at the end of the 19th century, led by Father Pierre Prudent Rene, and was completed in 1914. Its blue and white walls are visible to fishermen from the sea. Inside the church the atmosphere is calm, the temperature is definitely cooler and the wooden pews are inviting. Enjoy the scenery and a few moments of relaxation.

Open to the public from dawn till dusk all week (and never empty), the weekend mass is held on Sundays at 10:00 am.
Address: Church Street, Choiseul
Telephone: +758-459-3681

37. La Maison Creole

La Maison Creole is the most authentic museum of artefacts in Saint Lucia. Situated in Choiseul on the way to Vieux Fort, it showcases the traditional way of life of previous generations. On display are tools, pottery, clay pots, handmade furniture, crafts, old coins, musical instruments, woodcarvings, toys, a miniature traditional house and even an ancient boat. The centre is a project of the Ministry of Education to encourage skills development and local arts.

Along the roadside in Choiseul you will find on sale items such as locally made coal pots (still widely used in Saint Lucian kitchens), mats, market chairs and other utensils. Few tour operators venture all the way to this side of the island, so hiring a vehicle or a private taxi tour for a day is the best option to visit the southwestern parts of Saint Lucia. La Maison Creole is open weekdays (except public holidays).
Address: La Fargue, Choiseul
Telephone: +758-459-9691

38. Balenbouche Estate and Heritage Site

Balenbouche Estate is a plantation and guest house popular with both visitors and locals for weddings and retreats. The estate is filled with character: large open grounds with cottages all around and the ruins of sugar mills. You can almost feel the souls of those who worked there tirelessly long ago. The Estate has an amazing garden, fruit orchards filled with the most beautiful flowers, the tallest trees filled with birds, cats and dogs milling around and beaches just a short walk away.

Balenbouche Estate is located in the south of the island between the villages of Laborie and Choiseul, about 20 minutes

from the International airport. Guided tours of the estate and main house are available on a regular basis during the winter.
Telephone +758-455-1244
Website: www.balenbouche.com

39. Moule a Chique Peninsula

Above Vieux-Fort, on the southernmost tip of the island, there is an old lighthouse that was built in 1912. Replaced by a modern unit, it has been restored for weddings and photo shoots.

The view from the top of Moule a Chique is one of the most spectacular in Saint Lucia. Facing the island of Saint Vincent and the Grenadines to the south where the Atlantic Ocean and the Caribbean Sea meet, the surrounding cliffs are home to numerous sea birds. Off the Atlantic shore to the east, Sandy Beach and the Maria Island Nature Reserve face each other. To the north, the panorama includes Vieux Fort's plains and Hewanorra International Airport, and beyond the hills, one can see the Pitons and even Mount Gimie — the highest point of the island's central mountain range.

40. Maria Islands Nature Reserve

Set to the east of Moule a Chique Peninsula in Vieux Fort, the islands are about half mile out from Sandy Beach (Pointe Sable). Maria Major (10.1 hectares) and its little sister Maria Minor (1.6 hectares) are home to more than 120 species of plants, lizards, butterflies and snakes. Both islands are surrounded by coral reefs: a snorkeler's paradise!

The Maria Islands were declared a nature reserve in 1982 in recognition of their unique flora and fauna. This wildlife habitat is home to some endemic reptile species: the Kouwés Snake (Saint Lucia Racer or Dromicus Ornatus), the Saint Lucia Whiptail (Zandou), the non-poisonous Worm Snake, the Pygmy and rock geckos. The island is also a major nesting site for West African migratory birds, such as the Sooty Tern, the Bridled Tern, the Caribbean Martin, the Red Billed Tropicbird, and the Brown Noddy. The reserve is usually closed for the nesting season running from May till August.

The Saint Lucia National Trust organises special guided tours to the Maria Islands Nature Reserve. Tours are given by appointment only.

For more information, contact the Saint Lucia National Trust.
Address: Maria Islands Nature Reserve, Vieux Fort
Telephone: +758-452-5005
Website: www.slunatrust.org

41. Latille Waterfalls and Gardens

For this one, you have to travel just outside of Micoud Village on the east coast. Bordered by the rainforest, the property is privately owned and managed. The lush grounds are filled with blooming flowers, fruit trees and herb gardens. In addition, you'll find an enchanting 7-metre (20-foot) waterfall cascading into a deep swimming pool. The owner, who lives on site, generates power with a hydroelectric system.

Address: Latille Waterfalls, Mahut Micoud

42. Des Cartiers Rainforest Trail

To reach the Des Cartiers Rainforest Trail, you will have to travel on the East Coast Road to Micoud Village. Just north of Micoud, you turn inland to the west at the signpost. The 6-mile (9 km) drive to the trailhead takes around one hour, and passes through the small village of Anbre. Once you arrive at the Interpretation Centre, a fee of US$10.00 per person (half price for kids) is payable to start the trek.

This easy loop trail is 2.5 miles (4 km) long, and it takes two hours to complete. Red Anthuriums grow along the path as you head into the high-canopied rainforest. Several observation points are found along the trail, allowing visitors to spot all endemic bird species residing in the Forest Reserve, such as the famous Amazona Versicolour. Situated at 550 metres (1,800 feet) above sea level, the reserve receives 380-500 cm (150-200 inches) of rain annually. Come prepared!

The northern part of the loop trail links up with the Edmund Forest Reserve through the Quilesse Forest Reserve Trail: you need a guide for this four hour hike to the west coast.

The Interpretation Centre is open Monday to Friday from 8:30 am to 2:00 pm. Call the Forestry Department for further information (+758-468-5645/5648/5649).

43. Frigate Islands Nature Reserve Trail

Between Micoud and Dennery, just off the east coast, the Frigate Islands are a cluster of rocks a short distance offshore from Praslin Bay. The islands were named after the Scissor Tailed Frigate birds (Fregata Magnificens) that breed here between May and July.

The Frigate Island Nature Reserve Trail is a kilometre hike through rich vegetation, including mangroves and yards-high cacti. Visitors arrive under guided supervision at an observation post looking out over the islands. Closed during the breeding season from early May to the end of June, tours can be booked through the Saint Lucia National Trust.

Address: Frigate Islands Nature Reserve, Praslin
Telephone +758-452-5005
Website: www.slunatrust.org

44. Mamiku Gardens

Situated in Praslin, near Mon Repos Village, this botanical paradise is located just off the Atlantic Coast's main road. Mamiku Gardens is set on a 12-acre property surrounding the hilltop ruins of the Micoud Estate. Originally owned by Baron de Micoud in the 18th-century, a French Army Colonel who was Saint Lucia's Governor General, the estate was deeded to his wife, Madame de Micoud, to avoid confiscation by the British. Locals called her "Ma Micoud," which, over time, became "Mamiku". In 1796, slaves burned the estate down to the ground during the Brigand's War. It is now primarily a banana plantation.

The gardens are inspiring: the Mystic Garden, with its different species of orchids; the Secret Garden, with its butterflies and birds; Grandpa's Garden medicinal herbs sanctuary; and Veronica's Garden — perfect for weddings. Mamiku Gardens and the Madame de Micoud Ruins are an excellent place to photograph flowers such as Orchids, Heliconias, Anthuriums and Gingers. A short, slightly steep trail leads through the forest to the Madame de Micoud Ruins. There is an excellent view of Frigate Islands and Praslin's Port from the high vantage point of Tamarind Hill.

Mamiku Gardens are open seven days a week from 9:00 am until 5:00 pm. For a small fee, the site will arrange for a guided tour. When you are done, enjoy a drink by the Brigand's Bar.
Address: Mamiku Gardens, Praslin
Telephone: +758-455-3729

45. Errard Plantation

Situated in the vicinity of Dennery's village, visitors can only access Errard Plantation by joining an organised day long tour, which includes many activities. The convoy of open top Jeeps usually starts the journey from the north of Saint Lucia, collecting all the guests along the way from the different resorts. From Castries onwards, the drive will take you across the rainforest through Bexon and the Barre de L'Isle Ridge.

On the other side, the Atlantic Ocean suddenly appears between the hills. As you drive along the east coast, feel the sun on your skin and the wind in your hair. Last right turn by Dennery's river and you are almost there.

First discover the beautiful historical Errard Plantation House. It has been in the care of the Devaux Family for generations. Gary Devaux and his staff will cater for all your needs and answer all your questions in a joyous, uplifting atmosphere: in our opinion, the most hospitable team islandwide!

Step back in time as you stroll around this magnificent 300-year-old cocoa and coffee plantation. Learn why nutmeg was the last crop produced on the estate. You will experience the processing of cocoa beans with the "cocoa dance" and the drying of the nutmeg's mace. You also have the option to go walking through the rainforest and to enjoy its lush vegetation, home to a large variety of local birds and animals. After a delicious Creole lunch with local fruit juices, the afternoon ends with a refreshing swim in the nearby waterfall.

Advance bookings only, call for tour information.

Address: Errard Plantation, Dennery

Telephone: +758-453-1260

46. Fond d'Or Nature and Heritage Park

Located in the Mabouya Valley, north of Dennery's village on the east coast, the Fond d'Or Nature Reserve & Heritage Park has been promoted by the Heritage Tourism Association of Saint Lucia (HERITAS) since 1999. This site is definitely rich in history, culture and mythology, with a colonial sugar mill built over a former Amerindian settlement. In May, Fond d'Or becomes a concert venue during the Saint Lucia Jazz Festival.

A 45-minute moderate hike will take you through the vestiges of three technologies used for sugar production: wind, cattle and steam mills. The area includes a mangrove and woodland, with plenty of birdwatching opportunities. The beach is a nesting site for Leather Back turtles.

47. Saint Peter's Church

Located in the small fishing village of Dennery on the east coast of Saint Lucia, Saint Peter's Church stands above the entire village. Saint Peter was the obvious choice as he is the patron saint of fishermen.

The church was built in the late 18th century on a little hill facing the Atlantic Ocean. It stands out as the most imposing structure for miles around, and it is one of the designated shelters of the National Emergency Management Organisation (NEMO) for the local population during hurricane season.

Like all catholic churches in Saint Lucia, it is open to the public from dawn till dusk every day of the week. The weekend mass is scheduled on Sundays at 10:00 am.
Telephone: +758-453-3311

48. Barre de l'Isle Forest Reserve

Located in the centre of the island, the Reserve gets its name from the fact that it is a ridge that divides the eastern and western halves of Saint Lucia. The Barre de l'Isle Forest trail is a half hour drive away from Castries, going through the Bexon community in the direction of the East Coast. With a US$40.00 entry fee per person, the reserve is home to the Anolis Lucia tree lizard and five bird species endemic to Saint Lucia.

The first half of the trail is moderate and well-maintained. This mile-long trek takes about an hour to complete, winding through the rainforest and providing great views from four panoramic lookout points. It features views of Mount Gimie to the south, of the Mabouya Valley to the east, and of the Cul de Sac Valley to the west.

The second half is strenuous and optional. The forest is mainly composed of Pine, Blue Mahoe and Mahogany trees. Visitors opting to climb Mount La Combe (438 metres/1,404 feet) will add another hour to the trek, with even more breathtaking views and a good workout!

Open Tuesday to Thursday. Contact the Forestry Department for more information.
Address: Barre de l'Isle Forest Reserve, Barre de l'Isle
Telephone: +758-468-5645/5648/5649

49. Union Nature Trail and Mini Zoo

Situated just north of Castries (a 15 min drive away), you will have to turn inland at Choc Bay towards the east to find this attraction. This Agricultural and Research Station, used as a nursery, includes a hillside trail, a garden trail and a medicinal garden within its ecotourism services.

The Union Nature Trail is a looped trail that takes you through a secondary dry forest in just about an hour. Humming Birds, Finches and Warblers can be spotted along the way. In the medicinal herb garden, you can discover the wonders of the local "bush medicines" used as alternative therapies. Finally, the Mini Zoo features nine species of endemic wildlife, including Iguanas and Agoutis. Entry fee is US$40.00 per person. Contact the Forestry Department for information (+758-468-5645/5648/5649).

Fort Rodney, Pigeon Island

50. Morne Pavillon Nature Reserve

Located near the northern tip of Saint Lucia, facing Martinique, Morne Pavillon became a nature reserve when the landlord, Christopher Lutz, decided to donate the property to the National Trust for the preservation of this heritage site.

It was first named Morne Pavillon in around 1700 by the French Civil Commandant, Baron de Longueville, when he planted his flag at the top of the hill. It was at this time that the area became a cotton plantation. During the Second World War, the U.S. government leased the site for the construction and operation of a military base (200 men), including a 2 x 155mm shore battery. The goal was to protect the US Air Base at Reduit, and Saint Lucia, from possible invasion. In the 60's, the site was sold to a syndicate who began to develop Cap Estate, with the construction of up-market residential estates.

According to the Forestry Department for Wildlife, 22 species of birds can be observed on-site. The area is home to three endemic bird species: the Saint Lucia Pewee, the Saint Lucia Oriole and the Saint Lucia Warbler. 51 species of plants are also identified. The dominant tree species are White Cedar, GommierModi, Ti Bonm, BwaLanmowi, Campeche and Bwa Flambeau. Tours are not organised in the reserve on a regular basis. For more information, contact the Saint Lucia National Trust (www.slunatrust.org).

51. Pigeon Island National Park

Pigeon Island National Park is one of Saint Lucia's most important historic attractions. First occupied by the Amerindians, in the 1550s it was a hideout of the notorious French pirate François le Clerc (also known as Jambe de Bois on account of his peg leg). The British used the land to house a garrison from which to observe the French activities in neighbouring Martinique and there are forts standing on both summits.

This 44-acre site was once an island accessible only by sea, but a causeway was built in 1972 to join it with the mainland. In 1979 the Government of Saint Lucia designated Pigeon Island a National Park and then upgraded that status to a National Landmark in 1992. It has been restored by the Saint Lucia National Trust as a landmark encompassing all aspects of a rich historical heritage, for educational, cultural and recreational purposes.

Grasslands, dry tropical forest and beaches are the geological points of interests of the park. Visitors can hike up to the lookout point and enjoy panoramic views of Saint Lucia's northwest coast and Martinique. Today, it has become the centre stage venue for the annual Saint Lucia Jazz Festival, held in May. The park offers the following attractions and amenities: for a small entry fee (US$7.00 for visitors; US$1.50 for children 5-12 years old), an interpretation centre tells you the story of Pigeon Island, and visitors have access to two restaurants and a couple quiet white sand beaches.

The Park opens from 9:00 am to 5:00 pm and guided tours led by experienced tour guides can be arranged. Call for further information.

Address: Pigeon Island National Landmark, Rodney Bay
Telephone: +758-450-0603 or 452-5005
Website: www.slunatrust.org

52. Saint Joseph the Worker Church

Situated in the north of the island, the Saint Joseph the Worker Parish was created in 1763 under the guidance of Abbe Termoniac, the first recorded priest in Saint Lucia. The Saint Joseph the Worker Roman Catholic Church's construction began in 1850 and was completed in 1876. Later on, the 1906 earthquake destroyed the building entirely. Finally, in 1927, the present church was built on the site of the old church, within walking distance from Gros Islet's main street.

It is another one of the shelters designated by NEMO for the local population during hurricane season. Today, the entire parish of Gros Islet comprises around 22,000 people, of which 17,600 are Catholics.

Also open to the public from dawn till dusk all week, the weekend masses are scheduled on Sundays at 8:00 am and 10:00 am.

Telephone: +758-450-8325

53. Antillia Brewing Company

The Antillia Brewing Co. is located just off the main road in the Rodney Bay Village, within walking distance from Baywalk Mall or any of the hotels in the area. It is the only craft brewery in the region. This local brewery specializes in traditional hand crafted fine ales and stouts, designed specifically for the climate and tastes of Saint Lucia. Andrew Hashey, the owner and brewer has more than 20 years experience in the world of craft brewing in Canada.

Three styles of ale are currently produced on a regular basis: Golden Wheat, Pale Ale and Stout. Antillia's brewer is also experimenting with ale flavoured by island fruits and barrel aging. Antillia's ales are served draft style at the brewery's taproom. A light fare bar menu, which goes perfectly with their brews, is available as well. Open daily from 11:00 am to 11:00 pm.

Address: Rodney Bay Villa, 4 Seagrape Avenue, Rodney Bay
Telephone: +758-458-0844

54. Stony Hill

There is much to recommend the wonderful village of Rodney Bay, so why not top it off with a majestic view from the Hills of Monchy? There are many things you may plan to do when you travel — maybe have a romantic wedding, enjoy the most memorable party of your life, or even pop the big question?

All this and more can be done in the most elegant and breath-taking garden overlooking Rodney Bay, the Marina, Pigeon Island, the Caribbean Sea and rest of the northern countryside. There is ample potential for adventure and it is yours to create and embark upon on the grounds of Stony Hills. Stony Hill hosts and caters for various local, social and business events. Whether with friends, your spouse, or the family, this spot provides the opportune moment to reminisce about your experience in Saint Lucia as you overlook it all.

Stony Hill's garden is nothing short of inspiring. Take a guided tour around the premises, enjoy some soulful music, learn about some of Saint Lucia's exotic flora and end with a cool beverage made from the fruits within the very garden!

Telephone: +758-458-0461/484-1137

Website: http://stonyhillstlucia.com

55. Lushan Country Life

Meet Arthur — Arthur Anthony — the man who turned a passion for sharing his country with tourists into a family business that now keeps all of the Anthonys busy! What began as an informal stop on his island tours has become a major attraction in its own right, as the family transformed their seven-acre property into a celebration of the history, nature and food of the island.

Explore the nature trails and discover beautiful trees such as Mahogany, Blue Maho, White Cedar and more. Visit the Herbal Gardens and find out what herbs and spices Lucians use in their cooking. Finally, watch as local food is cooked using traditional methods on an open fire.

Lushan Country Life also offers a day tour for cruise passengers, which includes the Lushan Country Life Estate, a trip to the beach at Rodney Bay and shopping in Castries Market.

Telephone: +758-451-6091 or 715-5402

Email: info@StLucia-Tours.net

Website: www.stlucia-tours.net

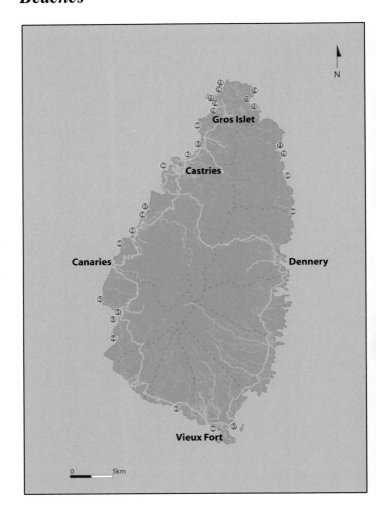

56. La Toc Beach

Leaving Castries and heading towards the Millennium Highway, go west past the Ferry Terminal. The road winds a bit, and taking your fourth right will put you on the road that has access to the crescent-shaped La Toc Beach, a gorgeous stretch of powdery white sand and calm waters, which make it very suitable for swimming and other beach activities.

The atmosphere is relaxed, perfect for sunbathers, beach walkers and casual swimmers. The sand looks as though it's been plated in gold and shimmers spectacularly in the sultry island sun. Off to the left is a small bluff jutting out into the water.

With a wide choice of exciting sites nearby on Morne Fortune, such as the Government House, you'll never run low on things to do. Among them, historical attractions such as La Toc Battery offer a nice compliment to a soothing day at La Toc Beach, and provide beachgoers with the opportunity to learn about Saint Lucia's past, without having to venture too far from the coast.

The beach can be publicly accessed through the resort or by boat. A concession stand is located to the left side of the beach and food can also be bought from one of the local vendors around. Sadly, there are no public restrooms available and this fact should be taken into consideration if you are planning to visit.

57. Marigot Bay

Heading south on the West Coast, through the Cul-de-Sac Valley with its endless banana plantations and toward the Roseau Valley, you will come to Marigot Bay, one of the most secure anchorages in the Caribbean. Here you will find an oasis of calm, with a wide range of sophisticated accommodation, bars and restaurants, and both water and land-based vacation activities. The beach itself is located across the bay from the access road, so a ferry or water taxi is needed to reach it.

Described by American Novelist, James A. Michener, as "the Most Beautiful Bay in The Caribbean", Marigot Bay was the setting for the movie Doctor Doolittle – the original film starring Rex Harrison. Considered an up-market and exclusive destination, Marigot Bay has been a favourite Caribbean yachting destination for over 50 years – with a marina and berthing and service facilities to support nearly every type of yacht.

The beach itself is quite small but makes up for this with its serene atmosphere and picture-perfect image: the water is clear, extremely calm and pleasantly shallow for quite a distance out, while the brilliant white sand is lined with coconut palms. Should you tire of this view, a variety of activities are available, including scuba diving and deep sea fishing, hiking trails and birdwatching, spas and exercise classes, as well as excursions by boat or taxi.

Lounge chairs are available for rent and there are beach huts selling food, refreshments and local crafts. There is also a shop near the beach's dock renting gear for snorkelling. Unfortunately, there are no public restrooms available, but thankfully parking is available along the road near the dock.

58. Roseau Bay

Continuing south along the west coast you will meander through the Roseau Valley with banana fields on either side. Halfway through the straight and flat road, you will meet Roseau Village on your right. To the left, the community of Millet is the location of the renowned Circle River Trail, one of the Heritage Tourism Programme's main attractions. The highlight of this trail is the Venus River that winds through Millet, all the way down to the Roseau Valley. This is an easy trek and it includes an exceptional freshwater bathing area.

To the right and beyond the village lies Roseau beach. The shoreline is reached via a road through the banana plantation and behind Saint Lucia Distillers, the rum production facility in Roseau (four-wheel drive advised). Once on the beach you will be captivated by the landscape of Roseau Bay, nestled between two steep green-forested hills. In the middle, a river gracefully meets the sea, while on the left a puzzle of streams blend into the vegetation behind the sandy shore. The empty shacks scattered about the beach further give it that relaxed Caribbean feeling.

It is an isolated location with no amenities and seldom used by the locals. For this reason, a visit here is not advised without a local registered guide.

59. L'Anse La Raye

The fishing village of Anse-la-Raye, situated in a cove at the foot of steep hills, is blessed with freshwater from two rivers that end their course in the bay.

This picturesque beach, usually decorated with colourful traditional fishing boats, is great for relaxing and watching the local fishermen conduct their trade. For the divers, it is known as one of the finest wall and drift dives in Saint Lucia. All amenities can be found around the beachfront.

Last but not least, the Friday night fish fry is the 'not to be missed' event in the area. The fish fry first started a decade ago. Local seafood remains the staple of the fry, with everything from King Lobster to delicious Red Snapper on the menu. And yes, rum is still available, in addition to some lovely cold beers! Live music is still a big part of the event, with the calypso rhythms being played out all night.

60. Anse Couchon

There are many excellent snorkelling areas in Saint Lucia, some better known than others, but one of the locations most favoured amongst locals is Anse Cochon.

The road from Anse-la-Raye meanders and swirls around the hills towards the fishing village of Canaries, and after a short distance you will find, on your right, the entry to a steep track (four-wheel advised) leading to the Ti Kaye Resort & Spa, which stands guard over the secluded Anse Couchon cove below.

The beach is 200 metres long and its shores are covered with a mixture of volcanic dark and white sand. It is also accessible by boat, and the shallow reefs that begin very close to the beach make it one of the most exceptional snorkelling locations on the island. It offers a densely populated section of the ocean and is ideal for anyone with only a limited amount of time to go snorkelling while visiting Saint Lucia.

You can rent sun loungers, kayaks and snorkelling equipment from the hotel and there is also a restaurant right next to the water, to the left end of the beach.

61. Soufrière Beachfront

Continuing on south, passing through Canaries and Belvedere, this is the most challenging part of the rainforest road to Soufrière, the original capital town of Saint Lucia, founded by the French in the 18th century and filled with natural and historic sites.

As you descend and finally reach the sea again, the Soufrière Beach stretches out on your right the whole way along the waterfront, from the cemetery to the southern part of the city. This sand is brown and it is not one of the more popular beaches for tourists. On the other hand, Soufrière has numerous memorable spots to visit.

The most imposing landmarks are the towering twin peaks of the Pitons (see #22), which thrust up from the water to heights of over half a mile. While the peaks appear to be next to each other, one in fact rises south from Soufrière (Petit

Piton) and the other north from the fishing village of Choiseul (Gros Piton).

Not so far from the Pitons are the Sulphur Springs (see #23), a seven-acre crater named as the Caribbean's only drive-in volcano. Nearby, the Diamond Botanical Garden Waterfall (see #24) and Mineral Baths have to be mentioned. There are also a few estates, plantations and waterfalls in the surrounding area. Amenities are available at all sites mentioned above.

62. Anse Chastanet

As you drive into Soufrière, at the bottom of the hill, just before the cemetery and the town, take a sharp turn right onto another steep track in order to access two of the most exclusive and romantic resorts on the island: Jade Mountain and Anse Chastenet.

Anse Chastenet estate encompasses 600 lush tropical acres bordering two soft black sand beaches. Not only do you get a World Heritage Site anchored by the twin peaks of the Pitons on land, the resort's two crystal-clear bays are part of a designated marine reserve protecting miles of colourful coral reefs teeming with tropical fish.

A section of the beach has been roped off to prevent boats from disturbing the aquatic life allowing snorkellers to have a wonderful shallow water experience with some of the best underwater sights available in the entire world. The roped off area is now a nature reserve that has gained the title 'Fairy Land' because of the wondrous sights. Because the marine reserve is right off the beach in shallow waters it provides a unique environment that is great for underwater photography.

The beach is also accessible by water taxi. There is a dive shop where you can rent snorkelling equipment and the resort also rents out lounge chairs. There are showers positioned nearby the dive shop and bathrooms are also available for public use.

Anse Chastanet

63. Malgretoute Beach

Driving south from Soufrière town, before the volcano entrance, turn right down a very steep hill. When you reach the bridge at the bottom of the hill, there is a short track to the right (four-wheel recommended) leading to a beach with a mix of white and black sand and strewn with broken shells.

Malgretoute Beach is one of the lesser-known beaches in Saint Lucia, but the favourite of Stephane Terzuoli who wrote the Dive Guide at Appendix II. It is rarely crowded — especially true on weekdays — and offers a stunning diversity of underwater environments. Petit Piton towers above the beach to the south, and the scenery is one of a kind — in particular the sunset. A restaurant/guest house just above the south end of the beach offers many amenities.

In front of the central sandy part of the beach, the sea floor slopes gently for the first 10 metres, making it ideal for young children to snorkel and discover shoals of silver fish and colourful shellfish. Further in, the slope intensifies and the sandy floor houses an entertaining colony of small eels. The floor then falls away into the big blue ocean. At that point, you must beware of the strong currents at the change of tide.

On the south side of Malgretoute a shallow reef starts right at the beach and extends around the base of Petit Piton. The width of the reef plateau varies, as does the depth, as you swim south. From the edge of this underwater reef, the shelf falls away in a sheer drop thousands of feet below you. The moon-shaped scenery of the reef is the theatre of a tremendously active ecosystem: lobsters, moray eels, squids, octopuses, corals, sponges, and all species of Caribbean reef fish, from the smallest, to the biggest predators. It's a dream come true for experienced divers.

64. Anse des Pitons/Sugar Beach

Anse des Pitons, also known as 'Sugar Beach', sits between the Pitons and can be accessed either through the Viceroy Resort or by boat. Once covered in black sand, this beach is now shimmering white thanks to the Viceroy Resort, which imported it for their beachfront. The Resort plays a part in keeping the beach clean and supplies lounge chairs on the right side of the beach for the public to use freely. Some water sport rentals are available and a section of the water to the right-hand side of the beach is reserved for snorkelling.

65. Laborie Beach/Rudy John Beach

Back on the main road from Soufrière you will pass the village of Choiseul, Lafargue's Arts & Craft Centre, Balembouche Estate, River Doree, and Piaye's Village, before you reach the fishing village of Laborie. Here, they specialise in lobster conch, plucked straight from the clear turquoise waters of the Caribbean Sea. Mostly frequented by locals, this white sand beach extends far beyond the village and there is ample parking nearby.

Parallel to the beach, 60 metres out to sea, is a long, beautiful reef surrounded by shallow water, almost unknown to most Saint Lucians. On the beach is a small guesthouse where food and drink are available, and further on there are many restaurants and bars to be found in the village of Laborie.

One of Saint Lucia's best kept jewels, Rudy John Park is a joy for all to visit. It has a bay that is ideal for relaxing and swimming and the most wonderful reef, surrounded by shallow waters to please the avid snorkeller. With the new interpretation centre, Papel Arts & Craft Centre, there is a lot to see and learn. Food and drinks are available and there are washrooms onsite. Rudy John Beach Park is also now one of the Jazz Festival's free beach-side concert destinations.
A truly picturesque place to visit!

66. Vieux Fort

Clinging to the Moule-a-Chique peninsula on the southwestern coast of Saint Lucia, with its grey sand and clear water, this beach is not as popular with visitors as are others in the area. Yet it is a location appreciated for its proximity to the town of Viuex Fort and the laid-back atmosphere. There are no public bathroom facilities available on this beach, but food may be purchased from the local vendors who frequent the beach.

From the lighthouse at the end of the Moule-a-Chique peninsula, you can see the volcano in St Vincent, less than 50 km away. The cliffs are home to numerous sea birds. About half mile off the Atlantic shore is the Maria Island Nature Reserve, home to the endemic Saint Lucia Racer, a small nocturnal snake, and a ground lizard called the Saint Lucia Whiptail. It is a popular nesting area for migratory birds and for this reason the reserve is closed during nesting season (usually May to August). Tours can be booked at other times.

67. Anse des Sables/Sandy Beach

On the eastern side of the Moule-a-Chique peninsula, Anse de Sables ("sandy beach") is exposed to the fresh and reliable trade winds that it faces — a fact that has made it popular for windsurfing and kitesurfing. Windsurf boards can be rented on this beach and there's an excellent beach cafe called 'The Reef' where you can purchase food and drinks. This is a must-visit for any wind- or kitesurfing enthusiast.

Though windy, the beach is protected by reefs and the wide open bay is entirely sandy underfoot, making it one of the finest and longest beaches on the island. The beach is conveniently close to the town of Vieux Fort, and all amenities are available, with many establishments in close proximity.

You cannot fail to notice the Hewanorra International Airport, which sits like a lid on top of the funnel created by the mainland and the peninsula. In common with other volcanic islands, Saint Lucia has precious little flat ground on which to land aeroplanes. Hewanorra is the larger of two airports, with the George F.L. Charles Airport located in the north near the capital.

East Coast Beaches
Once you exit the Vieux-Fort area the coastline changes. The conditions of the Atlantic coast are radically different to those on the eastern coast. Usually, only local people venture on these beaches. Even for the most adventurous and experienced swimmers or divers, I would not advise venturing out unsupervised on any of the beaches located between Sandy Beach and Cas an Bas. It's also worth mentioning that the East Coast is the common habitat for all of Saint Lucia's native species of snake, as it is less populated!

68. Anse Louvet
Publisher's note: This beach is quite remote, difficult to access and you are unlikely to get a mobile phone signal. We strongly

recommend that you seek advice from local guides and tour operators.

Anse Louvet is on the eastern coast of Saint Lucia and with the road no longer driveable from the town of Au Leon, reaching this remote area will take a two or three hour hike. The beaches, each littered with coconut palm trees, showcase some breathtaking coastal views and features. The waves can be seen thrashing against the jagged coastal cliff sides, creating amazing blowholes.

Leatherback sea turtles come ashore to nest their eggs on these beaches and the area is also home to the only venomous snake on the island, the Fer de Lance. Anse Louvet's ocean waters are usually rough because it rests on the Atlantic side of the island, and so caution should be taken if you decide to go in the water. If you have time left to explore, a waterfall nearby the beaches can be reached by following the river into the main valley.

69. Grande Anse

To get to Grande Anse bay from Castries requires a long journey across the largest part of the island – but that's half the fun! The scenery is astonishing as you drive over the hills and through the villages of La Croix Maingot and Garrand, before reaching the hills of Desbarra and the stunning view of the island's rugged east coast.

Grand Anse is a beautiful bay, covered with fruit trees and home to the local wild pigs. The beach itself is the largest stretch of fine white sand on the island. However, the currents are very strong and it is dangerous to swim. Instead, one of the main attractions of this beach is that it's a popular site on the island for nesting turtle, due to its location. It is frequented by species such as the Green Turtle, the Loggerhead, the Hawksbill and the massive Leatherback. Nesting season runs from February to October, and turtles normally lay their eggs at night.

There are no amenities here, but there are two huts on the beach which can provide shelter should it rain. You should consider the assistance of a registered tour guide, or take an organised tour; four-wheel drive may also be necessary, especially during the wet season (June to October).

70. Petit Anse & Marquis Bay

From the village of Desbarra, drive back down the hill towards Garrand. Turn right at the intersection with the Bogis River. If Grand Anse is difficult to access, these two beaches are even trickier, and you have to leave even your four-wheel drive vehicle and finish on foot. Petit Anse and Marquis Beach are good spots for catching mud crabs and are also turtle nesting sites. Both are black sand beaches with no amenities. Swimming is not recommended due to strong undercurrents.

71. Dauphin Beach

Dauphin beach is reached by four-wheel drive vehicle from the village of Monchy. Though located on the eastern coast, the beach is shielded from the full force of the Atlantic Ocean and protected by high cliffs on both sides. Surrounded by lush greenery, the beach is made up of black sand and pebbles. The Amerindians who once settled in the area have left stone carvings and other physical reminders of their early presence. The ruins of a colonial church tower can also be found here, and these are the only remains of a town that was demolished during the French Revolution in the 1700s.

72. Anse La Voutte

More commonly known to the locals as the 'five-dollar beach' due to the $5 per person entry fee, Anse La Voutte (or Cascafe Beach) is a 20-minute drive from the town of Gros Islet, though a short downhill hike may be required at the end, depending on the road conditions. The hillside leading down to the beach boasts one of the most amazing vistas the east coast has to offer, with stunning views of the Atlantic Ocean breaking against the two reefs that protect the bay and a small island peninsula in the distance.

The beach is popular with some locals on Sundays and bank holidays, but otherwise will be nearly deserted. In spite of the entry fee, there are no amenities of any sort, but perhaps the soft golden sand and peaceful setting make it well worth the outlay! Beware of the strong currents at the change of tide.

Arch in Cul de Sac Bay on the south side of Morne Fortune

73. Cas En Bas
Cas En Bas beach is another outstanding location for wind- and kitesurfing, due to its accessible location, the reliable trade winds from the northeast and an outer reef that ensures that the shallow water is always flat. It is thus suitable for kitesurfers of all levels, as well as families with small children, or less confident swimmers.

Located a mere 10 minutes or so from Gros Islet, this wide, mile-long beach sits in the back of a c-shaped cove surrounded by hills covered in mangrove vegetation. Aquaholics Kitesurfing School operates from Cas en Bas beach, with gear for rent and kitesurfing lessons available. Kayaks are also available. Back on Cas-en-Bas road, Trim's Riding Stables offer a gentle horseback ride from the stables to the beach, along the shore and back to the stables.

For food there are a few restaurants based on the beach, Marjorie's being a highly recommended place to have a meal. Unfortunately, public restrooms aren't available.

74. Donkey Beach
Just around the northern side of the cove, Donkey Beach is generally quieter than Cas en Bas and sees less tourist traffic. It's popular with locals but you'll need a four-wheel drive vehicle to reach it; otherwise be prepared for a long walk.

75. Anse du Cap Beach
Leaving the Atlantic coast, we turn to the northwestern side of the island. Anse du Cap is a lovely black sand beach with very calm waters. Just above the beach is the Body Holiday at Le Sport Resort (all-inclusive of course).

Anse du Cap is located in Cap Estate, an old 1,500-acre sugar cane plantation that is dotted with some of the finest homes and hotels on the island (including several rental villas). At the centre of the Estate is the 18-hole Saint Lucia Golf and Country Club.

76. Anse Becune
Back on the Cap Estate main road, but going south, you will have to drive past the two roundabouts to find on your right the entrance of the Smugglers Cove Resort and Spa.
Anse Becune is another black sand beach that is quite large and good for snorkelling. No amenities can be found there, but the Cap Maison hotel is nearby.

77. Pigeon Island
Even without its beaches, Pigeon Island National Park would be a must-see attraction and is described in more detail at #51.

There are two small strips of beach located inside the park (entry fee required) and a large, more popular beach outside it.

The beaches have calm and clear waters that offer a good opportunity for various activities, such as swimming and snorkelling. The south beach waters are very calm and perfectly suited for small children. In comparison, the north beach is usually beaten by the waves.

There are lounge chairs and snorkelling equipment for rent on the beaches, and just before the entrance gate to the park there are shacks located on the left where locals sell food and drinks. Inside the park are public bathrooms and accessible showers, and parking is available just outside it.

Pigeon Island Causeway

78. Rodney Bay

This long white sand beach starts from Pigeon Island on the south side of the causeway and stretches south all the way back to the Gros Islet beachfront. Since the resorts were built (The Landings and Sandals Grande), the beach's popularity among locals has seriously decreased. It used to be the favourite family outing on weekends and holidays, as the waters are usually calm and clear. It is really a continuation of Reduit Beach, but is separated by the channel access to the Rodney Bay Marina and its inner harbour. No public amenities are available on the beach.

79. Reduit Beach

This is the most popular beach in Saint Lucia, among both locals and tourists. Long stretches of white sand and calm waters, combined with a host of activities, the close proximity of various amenities and plenty of parking, make this a good attraction for the whole family. The beach is easily accessed via the Reduit Beach Avenue, found by turning left off the Castries-Gros Islet Highway from the direction of the capital, before you get into Rodney Bay proper. Just off the Highway you will find not one, but two shopping malls - Baywalk and JQ's.

Located right on the beach are the Saint Lucian by Rex and the Royal by Rex resorts, both of which provide water sports equipment and lounge chairs for rent. There are no public facilities, such as bathrooms or showers, to rinse off.

Activities on offer include jet skis, parasailing, water skiing and more. With all the marine traffic, a snorkeller must be diligent about safety, and the south side of the beach is generally less busy. This area offers a great underwater experience and is especially convenient for those keen snorkellers who may be traveling with others more interested in what's above the water.

80. Labrelotte Bay

This crescent-shaped bay extends from the East Winds Resort to the Windjammer Landing Resort. Deep blue waters rush along the tan-coloured sands and there is a roped off section for swimming. It is suitable for water sports, and equipment can be hired at the resorts. The beach has a nice pick of restaurants and Jammer's Beach Bar and Grill is a great place to start.

Parking is available close by, but public bathrooms are not available on this beach.

81. Choc Beach

This gorgeous stretch of white sand is lined with majestic coconut palms that offer small oases of respite from the blazing tropical sun. The smooth blue waters are peaceful and great for swimming and snorkelling, and the picturesque Rat Island lies just off shore. It is easily accessible from the Castries-Gros Islet Highway, which runs almost parallel with the southern half, but the northern part of the beach is quieter, being as it is further away from the hustle and bustle of daily traffic.

Sandals Halcyon Resort and Villa Beach Cottages are located on the southern end of the Choc Bay (the Sandals Pier Restaurant is shown in the picture on the previous page) and the Wharf restaurant is conveniently positioned right in the middle. Water sports equipment is available for rent, but loungers are not. Although there are no public bathrooms on the beach, it is relatively close to Gablewoods Shopping Mall. An eight-theatre multiplex is located further up the highway, should the sun and heat become too much!

82. Vigie/Malabar Beach

Our journey around Saint Lucia comes to an end at Vigie beach, also known as Malabar beach, which is located right next to Castries. This is your second chance to sunbathe next to a runway (although the planes have a terrible habit of breaking the calm), in this case one belonging to the George FL Charles Airport.

The smaller of the two on the island, this airport is relatively quiet, with early morning, midday and evening flights. Its presence means a lack of hotels, which keeps the beach clean and peaceful.

The sandy shores of Vigie Beach slope gently into the clear blue waters of the Caribbean Sea, and it is well sheltered from unruly trade winds. A good variety of tropical trees can be found along the shore, including coconut palms, Seagrapes and Malabar almonds, creating natural and much-welcomed shade. At the southern end of the beach you can drive right under the trees and park beneath their shade. A few food shacks are stationed near the airport entrance and the public bathrooms on the airport grounds are the only ones nearby.

Being so close to Castries, you are in a good location for shopping or dining, if ever you should tire of sun, sea and sand!

CHAPTER 3

Activities

83. Street Party

The Gros-Islet Friday night street party is a perfect setting to sample the best of Saint Lucian cuisine, music and dance. Explore the various stalls and bars, and find something to your taste among the variety of fish, grilled meats and exquisite local beverages.

Visitors and locals alike congregate in the street and party to the rhythms of Jazz, Reggae, R&B and Dancehall music. If you're not much of a dancer or one to mingle, you can stroll along the waterfront, with views of the waves as they roll gently up and down the shore.

To first-timers it may seem intimidating with so much going on. Outgoing and friendly locals can be seen confidently roaming and dancing in the familiar streets, encouraging the more reserved visitors to relax and join the fun. Friday Night in Gros Islet is a unique experience not to be missed.

84. Seafood fiesta

Dennery Seafood Fiesta is much like Gros-Islet 'Friday Night' but with a change in theme — and that theme is 'fish, fish, fish!' The small fishing village of Dennery, not too far from the city of Castries, offers a more rural setting than its northern counterpart.

One of the benefits of this is that the fiesta is not so hemmed in by village houses. You can better appreciate the scenery as you dine on a table on the beach or dance to music. Enjoy a variety of fish dishes, as well as octopus, crab and lobster, to mention only a fraction of the menu.

85. Cricket

In common with most islands of the West Indies, cricket is strongly embedded in the island's culture. Saint Lucia is the birthplace of the former West Indies captain Darren Sammy, and up and down the island young and old can be seen playing the game on any given day, on grassy playing fields and sandy beaches. When an international match is being played, you can feel the excitement and tension in the air around the island as cricket lovers follow the action, glued to the television or radio.

The Beausejour Cricket Ground, only minutes away from the town of Gros-Islet and Rodney Bay, is the home of cricket on the island and hosted matches in the 2007 World Cup and 2010 ICC World Twenty20 competitions. Two matches from the WICB Professional Cricket League Regional 4 Day Tournament will be played in Saint Lucia from 11-14 December 2015 and 26-29 February 2016.

86. Football

On this island, sport is part of the lifestyle! Cricket plays a crucial role, but football is one of the most popular games on the island. Every town has a football ground, and as you drive around the island you might find a 5-aside small goals game or a full-blown match in progress. If you see crowds of people walking down the road, they are sure to be heading to a football game somewhere! Many of the hotels have their own football teams so if you are an enthusiast, why not ask to join in a local game? After a few minutes you will forget all about the heat!

87. Water sports

Ever heard of testing the waters? Well in the crystal clear waters of Saint. Lucia it is not simply an idiomatic expression! Numerous aquatic activities await your arrival on the sandy white shores, including snorkelling, kayaking, surfing, wind- and kitesurfing, stand-up paddling and even Snuba Diving. (That's not a typo – a cross between snorkelling and scuba diving, participants use hoses to breathe and can dive up to 6 metres (20 feet) beneath the surface of the water).

In Saint Lucia it's summer all year round! Friendly water sports attendants are always happy and willing to help you find an activity that is sure to match your skill level and expectations. (See Appendix III for a list of tour operators.)

88. Scuba Diving

Saint Lucia is well known for its diversity of marine life and pristine and colourful coral reefs. The warm and crystal clear waters surrounding the island are ideal for beginners and experts alike, and there are a number of dive operators offering short boat dives and night dives, as well as beginners' courses and advanced PADI certifications.

Saint Lucia enjoys average water temperatures of 26°C in 'winter' months and 28°C in summer. Conditions for scuba diving are great all year round, with visibility varying from 6 metres (20 feet) to more than 60 metres (200 feet), depending on the site and the weather conditions.

Be sure to have your camera ready and keep your eyes open for octopuses, turtles, flounders, urchins, needle fish and also a variety of corals, eels, parrot fish and lobsters. Highlights include diving at the base of Petit Piton or to the wreck of the sunken vessel called the Lesleen M. Without a doubt this underwater paradise is equal to the grace and beauty of the scenery above!

See Appendix II for guide to the best dive sites, Appendix III for a list of operators.

89. Catamaran cruise

Some time ago, I found myself on the "milk run": a flight from Antigua to Barbados that stopped in Dominica, Saint Lucia and Saint Vincent, before terminating in Barbados. Flying in and out of these mountainous islands on a small plane was quite an experience and it also provided great views of the stunning features of Saint Lucia (for those who were brave enough to look!).

The next best thing to flying over the island is viewing it from a boat. The distance gives you a better appreciation of the scale and beauty of Saint Lucia's unique topography. The Pitons, for example, seem to jump up out of the sea like two whales surfacing for air.

In addition to sightseeing, cruises will offer swimming and snorkelling and also provide lunch. Some operators combine land-based tours with the cruise, enabling you to pack as much as possible into one day.

But of course, vigorous activity is completely optional in this island paradise; you're quite welcome to find a comfortable spot on the front of the boat, grab a glass of rum punch and simply relax, as the boat glides along the crystal clear waters of the Caribbean Sea.

See Appendix III for a list of tour operators.

90. Dolphin/Whale watching

Take your sightseeing to deeper waters and set off in search of whales and dolphins. While you are never 100 percent guaranteed to see whales, most sightings do occur at least 2 miles off shore. You will be looking for graceful giants of the sea, such as the sperm, pilot and humpback whales, as well as orcas, turtles and a variety of species of dolphin.

Some boats are equipped with hydrophones to enable you to hear the smartest mammals of the oceans as they chatter away in clicks, squeals and clacks. The whales love nothing more than to showcase their acrobatic skills, as they powerfully breach the surface of the water and come crashing down in a thunderous cascade of foam and surf.

See Appendix III for a list of tour operators.

91. Sports fishing

The deep waters around Saint Lucia are teaming with tropical fish, and harvesting this valuable natural resource has been an integral part of the culture for centuries. Fishing villages and communities are dotted around the coast of the island, providing a livelihood for a significant portion of the population.

Sport fishers from across the region and around the world flock to the island in search of blue marlin, sailfish, black- and yellowfin tuna, and barracuda. The seasoned fisher can choose a private charter, while group fishing excursions are available to novices. See Appendix III for a list of tour operators.

92. Golf

This beautiful island holds something for everyone, including an 18-hole, par 71 golf course. The Saint Lucia Golf and Country Club is located in Cap Estate in the northern part of the island and offers one of the most striking and challenging rounds in the Caribbean. Visitors are only required to indicate their interest 24 hours before tee-off. Enjoy the rolling, luscious green landscape as you swing through your rounds, and end with refreshments at the onsite bar and restaurant.

In additional, the Sandals Golf Club is situated just south of Castries, up the La Toc road. Nestled in a lush green valley, this 9-hole course is short yet challenging and offers stunning views across La Toc bay.

93. Water Park

Floating in the shallow waters of Reduit beach in Rodney Bay, Splash Island Water Park is one of the few places where you won't be able to resist your inner child. Go on, splash away as you revel in this wet, floating world of wonder! The water park consists of a trampoline, double rocker, flip, and water volleyball and the floating 'wall.' It also features several water sports activities, such as kayaking, tubing and a water taxi to Pigeon Point. Under the warm Saint Lucian sun, this water park haven is by far the highlight of a visit to Rodney Bay.

There are different pricing options, with hourly, half- and full-day passes available, as well as packages that include lunch. For more information and to book online visit www.stluciawaterpark.com.

94. Saint Lucia Segway

An adventure tour with a difference - learn how to ride a Segway, and then experience Saint Lucia in a unique way. Mounted atop your futuristic steed, you meander through trails specifically developed for this tour. With the help of expert guides, explore a 1.7-mile route through the historical treats of Mount Pimard, and learn about the many battles that were fought over this little country.

The Saint Lucia Segway Nature Trail features a two-hour tour around Rodney Bay. After a spin on Pebble Beach, riders go up Mount Primard to see a volcanic masterpiece and experience the "Stone Face Fish Pond" for a pedicure. On the descent, guests can enjoy panoramic views of Pigeon Island, the Rodney Bay Marina, and the Caribbean Sea.

The price is US$85.00 per person. Open Monday to Friday, 9:00 am to 11:00 am & 2:00 pm to 4:00 pm, Saturday & Sunday 10:00 am to 12:00 pm & 2:00 pm to 4:00 pm.
Address: Rodney Bay Marina, Gros Islet
Telephone: +758-458-9656
Website: www.tropicaldiscoveries.net

95. Treetop Adventure Park

Treetop Adventure Park is located in the district of Dennery on the east of the island. Feel the exhilaration run through your body as you zip line safely through the treetops of the tropical rainforest and view the landscape below in unparalleled style. There are activities for children, so no one is left out.

The adrenaline rush from zip lining through the canopy at speeds of up to 30mph, more than 150 feet in the air, is sure to leave you wanting more. You can also enjoy an entire day of treetop adventure activities and take a guided cycling or hiking adventure through the rainforest. Listen for the songs of the birds in the distant canopy, and keep your eyes open and cameras ready for possible exotic wildlife on the excursion. End the day with refreshments at your destination point.

Telephone: +758-452-0808
Website: www.adventuretourstlucia.com

96. Hiking

The endless countryside, hills, valleys and sandy coasts are nothing short of a hiker's paradise. The warm island provides the ideal atmosphere and terrain for hiking. Life teams within every nook and cranny of the tropical rainforest and coastal areas of Saint Lucia. Enjoy hiking on nature trails such as Tet Paul, the Edmund Forest trail and Gros Piton or Petit Piton. The climate is perfect for hiking all year round so your main necessity is your camera, as you take pictures of the incomparable panoramic views the island offers.

Learn about the exotic wildlife, plants, trees and fruits found in Saint Lucia. If you are a birdwatcher by hobby or by profession, listen as you are serenaded with the songs of various species of birds in the treetops. With the most experienced guides, get a chance to see wildlife such as the indigenous iguana in its natural habitat and enjoy the majestic beauty of Saint Lucia.

See Appendix III for a list of tour operators.

97. Horseback riding

There are three stables that offer horseback riding tours and lessons on the island: Hoof Print Horse Riding Ranch, International Pony Club and Atlantic Shores Riding Stables.

You can choose from horseback riding through the banana plantations or down to the coast for a swim with your mount. To any appreciative and skilled horse rider the mountainous island can only be regarded as a treat as they put their mount to the test, while the less daring can enjoy a gentle canter along the beach.

See Appendix III for a list of tour operators.

98. Treasure Bay Casino

Feel like you have won the jackpot in coming to Saint Lucia? It may really be so if you have had the chance to visit Treasure Bay Casino. Rodney Bay is known for its nightlife adventure, restaurant seaside dining, clubbing, and its Casino. Treasure Bay Casino is one of the main attractions of the recently erected Bay Walk Mall in Rodney Bay.

To enter the Casino, you must be 21 years or older and must enrol into the Player's Club to in order become a member of the Casino. The professional Casino provides a truly sophisticated and amicable atmosphere for all its patrons. Players busy themselves in the abundance of games: approximately 233 slot machines and 22 table games.

Address: Castries-Gros Islet Hwy, Gros Islet

Telephone: +758-459-2901

Website: www.treasurebaystlucia.com

99. Saint Lucia Megaplex 8 cinema

Caribbean Cinemas is a chain of theatres that operate regionally across the Caribbean. The theatre is most definitely fun and ideal for families, couples and friends, visitors and locals alike. It is conveniently located on the Choc Estate, near the well-known Mega J Warehouse. The Cinema is equipped with eight screens and always has many movies to choose from.

Address: Allan Bousquet Highway Choc Estate
Telephone: +758-450-2727
Website: www.caribbeancinemas.com

100.Castries Market & Vendor's Arcade

Castries market is without dispute the most interesting, colourful and busiest structure — and focal point — in the town of Castries. Even if locals have no immediate need to purchase produce or crafts at the market, you can be sure they would embark on the trip just for the fun of it — simply to see old friends, hear the latest gossip or news, or merely to be amidst this absolutely festive atmosphere and social hotspot. More than a mere business place or social platform, the Castries market holds much history and importance for the people of Saint Lucia.

For decades, tradition has continued to be passed down to younger generations on the very grounds of the market. Learn the usage of some important herbs in medicines and in cooking, how to prepare spices, as well as the art of basket weaving and basic craft making. Be assured you will leave the market a wiser person, following a visit to a place so bustling with activity and information. To truly appreciate the atmosphere and have a relaxed and enjoyable experience, visitors may chose to go with a local guide who can clue them in on the happenings and trends of the market.

You may get hungry after all the sightseeing, shopping and walking. No worries: sit down to lunch next door at the food arcade, also part of the Castries market. Go ahead and sample sumptuous local dishes and cool beverages; maybe even finally discover a recipe in which to use an old spice you had sitting in the cupboard back home.

101.Chocolate Experience

With the conditions ideal for growing cocoa (hot, wet and humid!), the crop is one Saint Lucia oldest and most important, dating back to the 1700s. You will find cocoa plantation scattered around the island, including the Marquis Estate, Anse Mamin Plantation, Emerald Estate, Morne Coubaril Estate and La Dauphine Estate.

In 2006 Hotel Chocolat bought the 140-acre Rabot Estate, making it the only UK chocolatier to own its own cocoa plantation. The Estate is part of Hotel Chocolat's 'Engaged Ethics' Cocoa Programme. Working over 140 farmers around the island, prices are guaranteed to be 30–40% above the world market price of cocoa and farmers are paid within a week of selling their crops.

A few years later Hotel Chocolat decided to open an actual hotel and in 2012 the boutique "Boucan by Hotel Chocolat" opened on the Rabot Estate. Nestled in between the Pitons and surrounded by a cocoa plantation, the Boucan's six lodges are in high demand, so if you don't manage to get room there, the next best thing might be to indulge in their "Tree-to-bar Experience" (that's a chocolate bar, not pub bar!).

Begin with a leisurely stroll through the estate's lush green cocoa groves as you look for ripe cocoa pods to be harvested. As the tour continues you will learn all of the stages required to produce chocolate, including fermenting, drying and mixing. There's lots of tasting involved and by the end you will have made your very own chocolate bar to take home to show your friends. (Or maybe it won't survive the drive back to the hotel!)

The tour is available Monday to Friday (except bank holidays) from 9:00 and lasts for two hours.

Address: The Rabot Estate, Soufriere

Telephone: +758-572-9600 or 9601

Website: www.hotelchocolat.com/uk/boucan

APPENDIX I
Food & Drink of Saint Lucia
By Nelliane St Clair

The local cuisine of Saint Lucia is as diverse and dynamic as the mélange of people who inhabit the island and our dining tables are blessed with an array of meals that are continually being improved by new methods of preparation.

In Saint Lucia, food is not merely a means of nourishment or regarded as a necessity - it is an experience. Every single dish here packs a good punch of island flavour and is more often than not enjoyed in the midst of merrymaking and good cheer.

You will find an assortment of delicacies that are unique to Saint Lucia and, capturing the true essence of the island, are usually named in the Creole or patois vernacular.

As such, they may not be immediately recognisable to a tourist. This short guide will help you enjoy some of the local cuisine.

Fish & other seafood

We catch and enjoy a variety of fish, such as red snapper, dolphin (mahi-mahi), tuna, flying fish and kingfish. Flying fish is a delicacy and is more associated with the Creole Day festivities (a celebration of the Creole language and culture).

Another delicious fish that we enjoy is the "Coff", also a huge part of our Creole celebration. You may know it as boxfish — a fish with not much flesh. It is customary that the "Coff" be cleaned out and stuffed with a richly flavoured mix that is prepared differently, depending on who's doing the cooking.

But to speak of seafood without mentioning our famous Crab Callaloo would be a huge injustice. This is a crab soup that includes dumplings and ground provisions (yams, cassava, sweet potatoes, etc) and is, more often than not, very spicy!

Breadfruit & salt fish

Although our national dish is green figs and salt fish, breadfruit is another starchy staple which has earned its rightful place next to our coveted salt fish. You would have to search far and wide for a Lucian who does not salivate for this simple dish. Breadfruit is not prepared in any particularly way or with much fuss. Its starchy bread-like quality is perfect for the well-seasoned and savoury flavour of the salt fish. Of course, nobody eats a good breadfruit & salt fish meal without an equally satisfying cucumber salad.

Smoked Herring and Cucumber Salad

Nothing is more traditional than joining the saltfish and breadfruit with smoked herring. The smoked herring is cooked with onions and local peppers, and sautéed in coconut (or an alternative) oil. Add cucumber salad to this delightful savoury dish.

Dumplings & Cocoa Tea

You may have heard of both dumplings and cocoa tea independent of each other, but it is only in Lucia that you will find this undisputed combo. Just like most meals here, every household has a different way of preparing this dish, but the essence is exactly as the name suggests. Rather than boiling the dumplings in water, they are cooked and marinated in cocoa tea. As the cocoa tea boils, it permeates and gives life to an otherwise plain dumpling, transforming it into a heavenly delicacy. This is my personal favourite!

Farine & Avocado

You may have noticed that Lucians do appreciate a deadly combo. After all, no man is an island. Farine is what remains after cassava has been juiced. It could simply be prepared to a porridge-like consistency and complemented with a few slices of avocado. However, some people enjoy making farine and avocado balls, which is a little like meatballs but with these two delicious ingredients. It is no secret what a healthy choice avocado is, so you can enjoy this delicious dish without compromising a healthy diet.

Bouillon

There is no man, woman or child who doesn't burst into a happy dance after arriving home from a tedious day of work or school, only to discover bouillon on their stovetops. Bouillon is prepared with a medley of ingredients, including dumplings, ground provisions, local leafy vegetables, herbs and of course, a suitable meat. The more popular meats include lamb neck and pig tail, or you could enjoy the best of both worlds and enjoy a mixed bouillon.

Locally made Green Seasoning

I simply cannot speak of Saint Lucian food without mentioning the all too familiar local green seasoning. No Lucian kitchen is complete without its own unique blend of green seasoning. A household's green seasoning is comparable to the family's fingerprint; no two concoctions of herbs and spices are the same!

We do not make a habit of purchasing artificially produced flavouring. Rather, we combine onions, garlic, salt, local spices, herbs, hot seasoning peppers and sweet peppers, and without doubt, each family has a secret ingredient. This mix is left to marinate and is basically utilised in some way or the other to flavour every meal.

Beers
Arguably, no meal is complete without a good, cold beer. Two of the most sought after brews in Saint Lucia are Heineken and Piton beers. Heineken is brewed in our local brewery and has been praised as one of the cleanest and most faultless beers worldwide. The Piton Beer, named after our most famous attraction, is a preferred drink among many and has come to evoke a sense of national pride in many Lucians. Both beers have amassed a very loyal fan base both locally and regionally.

Spiced Rum
Spiced rum is most commonly known by its patois name 'Anba Kontwe', which translates to "under the counter". Any decent rum shop will have spiced rum under its counters. It is a medley of rum, cloves, cinnamon, nutmeg, local herbs, orange peels and everything nice. While you can find this concoction all year round, it is even more popular around Christmas time. Some persons even drink it as a solid remedy or preventative measure for the common cold (though I do not know of any medical evidence to support this!).

Bush Tea
Herbal tea, or bush tea, is made from leaves plucked from local herbal plants and left to brew in scorching hot water. These teas do not contain any caffeine and are usually sweetened with local honey rather than with processed sugar. Bush tea has

many therapeutic benefits and is used as a remedy for many mild illnesses. For example there is no tummy ache that a hot mug of bay leaf tea can't sooth!

Sorrel
A truly Caribbean Christmas is not complete without a glass of sorrel juice. The crimson red flower from the sorrel plant is used to achieve a strong delicious brew, which is flavoured with spices, such as cinnamon and cloves, as well as local honey. This delicious drink is characteristically a Christmas drink but can be served on any hot day on the island.

Creole Bread & Turnover
Creole bread, so termed not because it is baked with different ingredients to normal bread, but because it is cooked in a hand constructed Creole oven. Nowadays, commercially produced bread is more readily available, but it is well worth your while to scour the entire island to find yourself some Creole bread.

Turnover is not unlike bread in that it is basically bread dough adorned with a sweet coconut filling. This can be found in every local bakery, as it makes for a great snack in between meals. This is especially favoured among children, as it does well to satisfy a sweet tooth.

Golden Apple & Sauce/ Mango & Sauce
These are pickle-like snacks, made with golden apples, mangoes or generally any fruit with a sour flavour. The sauce is made with vinegar, salt and spices, which makes for a very healthy and satisfying light dish. While it could also be made with ripe fruits — which make for a sweeter consistency — it is generally prepared when the fruits are green to moderately ripe.

Dive Sites in Saint Lucia
By Stephane Terzuoli

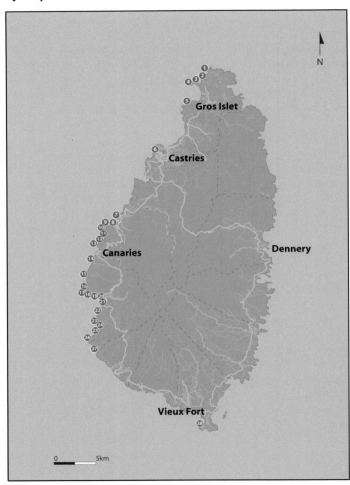

Before describing the many diving sites in Saint Lucia, I would like to advise all underwater enthusiasts to obtain travel insurance sufficient to cover any unforeseen events; the local health system requires that patients pay up front for any medical expenses.

Furthermore, in the event of a decompression accident, you would need to be flown to one of the neighbouring islands of either Barbados or Martinique.

All the diving sites are located on the Caribbean side of the island's coastline. I will start in the north and proceed south.

1. Saline Point
Located in front of The BodyHoliday Resort at Le Sport, this site is great not just for divers, but for snorkellers as well. Divers will see Scorpionfish, Pufferfish, shoals of grunts, rays and different varieties of eels. You can start from the beach in shallow waters. From 6 metres out it gets gradually deeper, with a maximum depth of 18 metres (59 feet)

2. Smuggler's Cove
Just north of the Smuggler's Cove Resort & Spa, you can enter this spot from the beach. Octopuses, lobsters and many schooling fish can be seen here amidst the rocks, the small caverns and the numerous coral heads. Flying Gurnards usually feed on the sandy patches.

3. Bird's Rock
Located north of Pigeon Point, this rock is also known as 'Bird Shit Rock', due to its popularity as the seagulls' first stop back from their daily fishing trip in the Caribbean Sea. Eagle Rays, huge Barracuda, Parrotfish, lobsters and many other tropical fish are found at this site.

4. Pigeon Point North
Dive sites to the north and south of the causeway are accessible from the beach on and are home to many varieties of fish, rock

crabs and lobsters. If you look carefully, you can find seahorses in the shallows. Trickier to access, the west cove on Pigeon Island has a small wreck, inhabited by sand eels and lobsters.

5.   Berger Rock - Barrell of Beef
Also known as 'La Roche' ("The Rock") this is a small island about a quarter of a mile outside Rodney Bay Marina. A flashing white navigational light marks this site, making it is easy to find on night dives. With a maximum depth of around 15 metres, this site is full of life, including shoals of Jacks, Snappers, Grunts, Kingfish and eels, Trumpetfish, Sergeant Majors and Brown Chromes. In the underwater trenches and valleys you will often see Triggerfish, lots of lobsters and Great Barracuda.

6.   Bone Yard
Located on the northern side of the mouth of Castries harbour, Bone Yard is the site of a World War II vessel and what seems to be an airplane's wing. The ship was allegedly torpedoed off the coast of Martinique and tried to make it to Castries Harbour. The wreck lies at 12 metres deep and is home to many lobsters and tropical fish.

7.   Anse-la-Raye Wall
Known as the "Bay of the Rays", this cove was once home to stingrays and eagle rays. The wall, which ranges in depth from 18 to 34 metres, offers a spectacular drift dive, rich in coral and marine life, from brightly coloured fire corals in the shallow areas, to purple vase sponges, barrel sponges and soft corals down deeper. Rays can be seen on the wall, along with turtles and schools of young Barracuda, Atlantic Spadefish, huge Pufferfish, Kingfish and Parrotfish. The wall is also home to Bristle Worms, Banded Coral Shrimps and Arrow Crabs.

8.   Anse Galet

Difficult to access from the road, this dive starts on the Anse Galet Beach, located to the south of Anse-la-Raye. The site is made up of a series of coral-covered rock fingers that rise from a depth of about 15 metres to just under the surface. Divers generally weave in and out of the fingers, as they slowly heads towards the point.

9.   Virgin's Cove

Virgin's Cove is a lovely reef dive that also offers a wall drift closer to the north point. It was named after a shipwreck that killed a party of nuns and is today commemorated by a cross erected on the point above the dive site. Shaped like a number '9', its maximum depth is around 21 metres. There are lots of large Barrel Sponges and brain corals, as well as the occasional Stingray, turtle, Atlantic Spade Fish or Barracuda that frequent this bay. Beware of the slight current closer to the points.

10. Rosemond Trenches

Shaped like the fingers of a hand, with valleys and trenches in between all covered with coral, the main feature of this dive is a 9 metre-long cave leading into a chimney that you can swim through. The trenches harbour Seahorses, Frog Fish, Turtles and a large shoal of Glassy Snappers. This dive takes around one hour, with a maximum depth of 11 meters. This is a "must do" dive in the Marine Reserve.

11. Anse Cochon

The "Bay of Pigs" comprises two diving sites on the northern and southern parts of the beach, both of which may be reached from the beach or from a boat. The north dive starts in as little as 1.5 metres of water and slopes away to around 18 metres. There are patches of coral and large fields of boulders and sandy areas. This is a great snorkelling site and divers regularly see turtles, Trumpetfish, Moray Eels, octopuses, squids and rays. In the south, the maximum depth is 12 metres and attractions include reefs, boulders, walls and pinnacles. This breeding ground is full of juvenile marine life and home to many flounders. The usual dive profile is one hour.

12. The 'Lesleen M' Wreck
This wreck is located in Anse Cochon, where a freighter was sunk in 1986 to provide an artificial reef. It sits upright on a sandy bottom at a maximum depth of 20 metres. The 51-metre long wreck can be entered through the engine room and is covered in soft coral and sponges: excellent habitat for juvenile fish and visited by many species of schooling fish. It is also inhabited by Soldierfish, Angelfish, lobsters, Moray Eels and Hawksbill Turtles. Take your camera!

13. Jambette Point North & South
Daggers' Bay is a lovely cove containing Jambette Point, but unfortunately gaining access from the main road is demanding and you are better off arriving by boat. The two sites possess a series of coral heads and are home to lobsters, seahorses, and many shoals of tropical fish. In the sandy patches, you can find rays, sand eels and Flying Gurnards.

14. The Daini Koyomaru Wreck
This Japanese dredger was sunk in 1996 to make an artificial reef and rests on its side, its width creating a wall to dive along. The wreck is mostly intact, but at a maximum depth of 33 metres, this dive is suitable for Advanced Divers only and ideal for Enriched Air (Nitrox). It is home to large French Angelfish, Horse-eye Jacks, Barracuda, Green Moray Eels, Snapper and a huge Puffer. Turtles can also be seen on this dive.

15. Turtle Reef
Named 'Turtle Reef' because of its crescent shape rather than the presence of turtles, you are still likely to see a few Hawksbill and Green Turtles here. The depth ranges from 12

metres to around 43 metres, and with lots of Pillar Corals and Barrel Sponges in the shallows, this reef attracts a wide variety of marine life.

16. Anse Chastenet Reef

Situated in the Marine Reserve, this reef lies just off the beach from the famous Anse Chastanet Resort. This spot is particularly nice for snorkellers and first-time scuba divers. The shallow reef is shaped like a plateau, starting at 5 metres deep and progressing to 18 metres, after which the face drops down to a depth of 60 metres. Covered with soft corals and Barrel Sponges, the reef is home to large Trumpetfish, chubs, Balahoos, Snapper and more than 150 other fish species, as well as turtles. It is a photographer's paradise!

17. Fairyland

Fairyland is located on a major headland and is sometimes subject to strong currents that keep the rich colourful corals and sponges very clean. Like most of the sites in the Soufrière area, it has a plateau shape, ranging from 12 metres at its shallowest to 60 metres at its edge. Turtles are often seen on this reef and are usually quite friendly.

18. Grand Caille

Grande Caille is a big rock located at the southwest end of a cliff, around 30 metres (100 feet) from the shore and reaching just above the surface of the water. There is a plateau all around the rock with a lip and the dive is a circular one around this massive reef. To the north of the rock, over the lip, it gets shallower where Fairyland is located. To the west and the south, over the lip, the dive drops into the big blue. To the northeast you have the shore with the cliff. And to the east, over the circular lip, lies the Devil's Hole site (see below).

19. Trou Diable

"Devil's Hole" lies between the Fairyland and Key Hole Pinnacles. Another plateau-shaped reef, with depths ranging from 12 to 30 metres, it has large finger coral, brain coral and Barrel Sponges scattered along its slope, housing Grunts, Blue Chromes and sand eels.

20. Key Hole Pinnacles

A stunning dive site with four spectacular coral mounds that rise dramatically from the depths up to within a few feet of the surface. The volcanic peaks are encrusted with black and orange Gorgonians, home to Trumpetfish, Filefish, Groupers, Jacks and Snappers. Seahorses are also seen here.

21. Ratchet Point

Ratchet Point is located near the famous bat cave in front of the Humming Bird Resort's beach. It is a very steep slope descending to 90 metres/300 feet. The dive includes Gorgonians and various types of hard corals. Occasionally, divers can see the rare Batfish.

22. Malgretoute

Just north of Petit Piton, this gorgeous black and white sand beach is the starting point for this dive. Enter the water at the end of the beach and simply make your way towards the Piton point. Southern Sennets, Jacks, Creole Wrasses and Grunts swim through the reef, their natural hunting ground.

23. Superman's Flight

This spot is named after a scene from the movie Superman II. Located to the south of Petit Piton's base, you can dive along a sloping wall reaching depths of 460 metres/1,500 feet. Famous for its strong current, this thrilling diving experience also features massive fluorescent sponges, large Gorgonians and various species of tropical fish.

24. The Piton Wall

Also found at the foot of Petit Piton, this spectacular wall dive starts at the shore and drops off to over 60 metres (200 feet). It is covered with Sea Whips, Gorgonians, delicate soft corals and lots of Feather Duster Worms. With lots of schooling fish, the spot also harbours seahorses, turtles and rays.

25. Jalousie

Situated close to Gros Piton's base, this reef slopes at about 45 degrees, and the bottom is mainly rubble covered with corals, Gorgonians and massive Barrel Sponges. Creole Wrasses and Jacks are abundant. Beware of the strong current!

26. Coral Gardens

Located at the foot of Gros Piton, the scenery is stunning both above and below the water. Suitable for snorkellers and divers alike, the depth ranges from 5 metres/15 feet to 27 metres/90 feet. Among the finger corals, you can discover lots of juvenile reef fish, as well as Triggerfish, Snappers, Barracudas and turtles. This garden will produce some spectacular photos.

27. The Blue Hole of Anse l'Ivrogne

This spot gets its name because when viewed from above, it looks like a hole in the ocean floor. Since the reef sustained severe storm damage a few years ago, it is rarely visited. However, it is an exciting deep dive with a very unusual entry.

28. Wawinet Wreck

Just off the Vieux-Fort coast, this site is possibly the best wreck dive in Saint Lucia. Sunk in the 1980s to make an artificial reef, it attracts large shoals of Grunts and Soldierfish. Unfortunately, only the most experienced amongst us can attempt this one because of the constant strong currents.

Appendix III
Tour Operators

Tours	Area code +758
Barefoot Holidays Saint Lucia www.barefootholidaystlucia.com	450-0507
Cosol Saint Lucia Tours www.cosol-tours.com	719-6697 / 450-6848
Cox & Company Ltd. www.coxcoltd.com	453-4362 / 285-7354
Exciting Tours www.climbgimie.wordpress.com	717-3172
Herod's Tours www.herodstours.com	716-6540 / 286-1282
Joe Knows Saint Lucia www.joeknowsstlucia.com	450-3847 / 717-1893
Real Saint Lucia Tours www.realsaintluciatours.com	486-1561 / 717-8604
Serenity Vacations & Tours www.serenitytvl.com	450-4525
Son of Man Sea Tours www.sonofmantours.com	519-5243 / 715-2748
Spencer Ambrose Tours www.spencerambrose.com	721-8844 / 584-1728
Saint Lucia Reps & Sunlink Tours www.stluciareps.com	456-9100
Typhoon Tours www.typhoontours.com	284-7575 / 518-3031

Watersports

Aquaholics Kitesurfing School www.aquaholicsstlucia.com	726-0600

Hackshaw's Charter Boats   453-0553
www.hackshaws.com

The Reef Kite & Surf   454-3418
www.slucia.com/windsurf

Saluna Watersports   518-8236
www.saluna-watersports.com

Tornado Kite & Surf Saint Lucia   713-2110
info@tornado-surf.com

Saintt Lucia Sea Trek Adventure   456-5006
www.facebook.com/SeaTrekSaintLucia

Sports Fishing

Captain Mike's Sport Fishing   452-7044 / 450-1216
www.captmikes.com

Hackshaw's Charter Boats   453-0553
www.hackshaws.com

Sailing Cruises/Catamaran Cruises/Charters

Captain Mike's Pleasure Cruises   452-7044 / 450-1216
www.captmikes.com

Destination Saint Lucia Ltd.   452-8531
www.dsl-yachting.com

Endless Summer Cruises   450-8651
www.stluciaboattours.com

Sea Spray Cruises   458-0123 / 452-8644
www.seaspraycruises.com

Saint Lucia Reps & Sunlink Tours 456-9100
www.stluciareps.com

Scuba Diving

Dive Fair Helen   451-7716
www.divefairhelen.com

Frogs   458-0798
www.facebook.com/frogsdiving

| Scuba Saint Lucia | 459-7755 |
| www.scubastlucia.com | |

| Scuba Steve's Diving | 450-9433 / 489-0411 |
| www.scubastevesdiving.com | |

Whale Watching
| Captain Mike's Whale Watching | 452-7044 / 450-1216 |
| www.captmikes.com | |

| Hackshaw's Charter Boats | 453-0553 |
| www.hackshaws.com | |

Horse Riding
| Hoof Print Horse Riding Ranch | 520-5102/489-3321 |
| www.hoofprintranch.com | |

| International Pony Club | 450-8665 |

| Atlantic Shores Riding Stables | 285-1090 |
| www.atlanticridingstables.com | |

About the Author
Russell Streeter was born in Barbados in 1979 to an English father and Guyanese mother. He grew up in the south east of the island and developed a love of the water and of sailing and swimming. It was competing in regional events in both sports that he was able to visit most of the islands in the southern Caribbean.

Russell is the author of the best-selling travel guide "101 Things To Do & Places To See In Barbados". He lives in England with his family and can be contacted at russell@101thingstodoandsee.com.